W9-AFO-277

SCHOOL LIBRARIANSHIP SERIES
Edited by Diane de Cordova Biesel

1. *Reference Work in School Library Media Centers: A Book of Case Studies,* by Amy G. Job and MaryKay Schnare, 1996.

Reference Work in School Library Media Centers

A Book of Case Studies

Amy G. Job
and
MaryKay Schnare

School Librarianship Series, No. 1

The Scarecrow Press, Inc.
Lanham, Md., & London

SCARECROW PRESS, INC.

Published in the United States of America
by Scarecrow Press, Inc.
4720 Boston Way
Lanham, Maryland 20706

4 Pleydell Gardens, Folkestone
Kent CT20 2DN, England

British Cataloguing-in-Publication Information Available

Library of Congress Cataloging-in-Publication Data

Job, Amy G.
Reference work in school library media centers : a book of case studies / by
Amy G. Job and MaryKay W. Schnare.
p.   cm.—(School librarianship series ; 1)
Includes bibliographical references.
1. School libraries—References services—United States—Case studies.
I. Schnare, MaryKay W., 1945– . II. Title. III. Series
Z675.S3J6   1996   025.5'2778'0973—dc20   95-42554   CIP

ISBN 0-8108-3098-1 (pbk: alk. paper)
ISBN 0-8108-3145-7 (cloth : alk. paper)

Contents

Foreword

The works in the School Librarianship Series are directed toward the library school professor, the library school student, the district supervisor, and the practicing library media specialist. The role of the school library media specialist as an agent of change within the educational system is a focal point for each of these volumes. The series will also explore the philosophical basis of school librarianship yesterday, today, and tomorrow.

It is my privilege to present a special book as the first title in this series. *Reference Work in School Library Media Centers* is a thought-provoking work that can be used in a variety of ways — for class discussion in a library school course, as a catalyst for conversations about policy at a state conference, or as a guide for a national committee on professional ethics.

The distinguished authors, Dr. Amy Job of New Jersey and MaryKay Schnare of Rhode Island, have developed a format that allows the user to study reference work in all of its aspects, grades K–12. Most of the material has evolved out of real situations: use it as a basis for discussions of policy or as a means to share insights with your colleagues.

Preface

While it has often been said that experience is the only satisfactory way to learn the art of reference work (Grogan, 1979), prospective and new library media specialists in today's world deserve all the assistance they can get. This book of case studies is designed to provide some of that aid in the form of sample problems that can arise in the school library media center in the performance of the duties traditionally termed "reference."

Integrating the use of the library media center into the curricular and extra-curricular activities of the school has always necessitated the interaction of the library media specialist, students, teachers and administrators. The library media specialist uses the reference and public relations functions to provide access to references both within and beyond the school and to aid users in learning the appropriate points of access for particular situations.

The functions usually called reference include those of readers' services, information services, selection of materials, and user instruction. Public relations includes the publicizing of the library media center's services and the preparation of bibliographic/mediagraphic and other resource materials. These functions are called upon daily in the school library media center as the media specialist serves as a resource and teacher for the school. As the concepts of whole language, inclusion, and enrichment become part of the school environment, so has the role of the school library media specialist expanded to provide resources for these approaches.

This work is divided into the three major levels of schools: elementary, middle or junior, and high or secondary school. The basic areas of reference functions are included under each, however, the problems are tailored to meet the needs of each level. Emphasis is placed upon the recognition that the basic skills are presented at the elementary level, and that without that basic framework, work with students at the higher level is virtually impossible, or at the least, very difficult. Attention has also been placed upon the differences between large and small and urban and suburban settings.

It is hoped that the case studies presented here can provide the prospective or new or even the experienced school media specialist with some insight into the many different situations that can arise in the media center during the interaction with students, teachers, and administrators as they search for information. Some suggestions as to possible approaches for handling each situation will be found in the various appendices located in the back of the book.

Acknowledgments

It is customary to give thanks to people who have aided others in need. In the case of this work, we feel especially indebted to the people at Scarecrow Press who believed us when we expressed our belief that a book of this type was needed. Special thanks go particularly to Diane de Cordova Biesel, our editor, who put up with our many delays and who asked the "right questions."

Gratitude is due also the many school librarians who gave us suggestions based upon their own experiences. Unfortunately, they are too numerous to list individually, but we hope they will accept our heartfelt thanks when they read the book.

Last, but not least, we must mention our appreciation to our families who encouraged our efforts and critiqued the studies. Their "reality check" was invaluable.

We hope the book will be of value to students and practitioners alike. We found it to be a challenging effort that expresses our philosophies of reference services. Librarians are known for sharing, and we believe this to be our contribution to the profession.

Introduction

"Books and job challenged in two censorship cases." "Montana meets the middle ages." ("Montana", 1994, p. 12). "Don't study witchcraft. Fire the librarian." So read some of the headlines dealing with cases that threaten school librarians. Censorship is a recurring theme in American educational history and can affect the quality of instruction provided by librarians, as well as their morale and employment status.

There is hope in this situation, however, in the form of informed educators who have prepared policies and procedures to counteract and, in some respects, eliminate censorship. School librarians need to be in the forefront of this effort and provide members of the educational community with the information and research skills that can insure a balanced approach to the selection and evaluation of literature and resources.

Reference services in the school library media center focus on the readers' services, information services, study, selection and evaluation of reference works, and user instruction. The school media specialist serves students of all levels, first through high school, and in all settings, from urban to suburban to rural. The realm of the library media center encompasses print and non-print and manual and electronic sources. It can be a center for learning, a place of fun, a source of materials for both research and recreation, and even a retreat for students who may require bibliotherapy assistance.

The following collection of case studies is designed to provide school library media specialists with glimpses into the world of school reference services. Hopefully, these will lead to discussions of both the practical and the philosophical aspects of reference service as students are prepared for their futures.

I. Elementary School Library Media Centers

A. READERS' SERVICES

1. PARENTS AS READING PARTNERS

The Johnson Street School, which is located in the lowest socio-economic area of the city, has four half-day kindergarten classes. Over the years, the classroom teacher and the library media specialist have noticed a decline in readiness for classroom activities. They have also realized that in spite of intensive literacy efforts on the part of the school department, the children lack materials in their homes and are not aware of the availability of resources through the local library and various parent centers. The library media specialist has written a grant to develop a program called "Parents as Reading Partners."

This program would bring small groups of parents and children into the school library on three consecutive late afternoons or evenings. The library media specialist would demonstrate reading a story to the children and then invite the parents to work with their own child, reading the same story again. At the conclusion of the reading time, each parent/child combination would receive a copy of the book used during that class, some related activities for the book, a box of crayons, some pencils and paper—both bond and construction. Refreshments would be served and the school social worker would be available along with the school nurse to assist,

1

answer questions, advise and so on. During the two successive classes, more story reading would then be modeled and more materials given away.

At the conclusion of the three-meeting event, parents would be asked to register with their child for a card at the local branch of the public library. Students and their parents would also be asked to visit the library on a regular basis and maintain a log of books they have read. Ten weeks after the last class meeting the logs would be brought to the school library and a graduation ceremony would be held. Students and parents would receive a certificate of completion and a copy of the current Caldecott winner.

Questions:

1. Would you fund this type of grant?
2. Is this type of community outreach more appropriate for the public library than for the school library media center?
3. Do you agree/disagree with the nurse and social worker being involved?
4. Should others be involved, such as the principal or the literacy people from the school department, or even the kindergarten classroom teacher?
5. Who, if anyone, should be involved from the public library?

2. STUDENTS AS WRITERS/ILLUSTRATORS

Mr. Fernandez is a new library media specialist at the Kennedy School. The school has long had a visiting author program. This program is funded through a business partner (the local bank), and seeks to bring in an author and an illustrator to spend a week with the students in a variety of activities—book talks, demonstrations of illustrations, revising stories the children have written, brainstorming ideas for writing and so on. The program requires a great deal of logistical work and is often disruptive to the normal routines of the building. Discipline problems seem to be on the rise during this week because of the number of children moving freely through the halls en route to the special author or illustrator activities.

Mr. Fernandez would like to become involved with this program, especially in selecting the authors and illustrators to be invited. He feels that many of the authors selected are not appropriate for the ages, interests, and reading levels of the students. Many of them are older authors and semi-retired. Many have not written or illustrated for the last several years. The bank, which funds the program, handles all of the selection and local arrangements with minimal input from the school. None of the teachers has ever expressed concern about the program but several parents have made comments at PTO meetings.

Although the school has a large ethnic population, no writers of color have ever been considered—nor have they been rejected. Mr. Fernandez feels that by pre-selecting in his own mind a number of authors and illustrators and promoting their works to the students and teachers, he can begin to raise the school's consciousness about authors of color. From there, he will begin to talk with the people at the bank, the PTO and the principal about having more of a mix of authors and illustrators in the program.

For the first semester, Mr. Fernandez selects about ten authors and illustrators to promote for the year. He uses some of his funds to purchase their materials, hangs up posters and creates bibliographies for students, parents and teachers. Mr. Fernandez does book talks or reads stories written by some of these authors. Together with the art teacher, he creates a program where students illustrate their book reports in the style of one of these illustrators. Further, he has created an interest in having at least two of the authors and illustrators come to speak at the school.

Questions:

1. What is Mr. Fernandez's next step?
2. Should he send the bibliographies of the "targeted" authors and illustrators to the bank?
3. Should he continue working away quietly from within as he has been?
4. Should he involve the PTO?
5. What role does the principal play in all of this?
6. Has Mr. Fernandez behaved in a less than professional manner by working behind the scenes to achieve his own aims?
7. What is Mr. Fernandez's agenda?

3. RECREATIONAL READING CENTERS

Newtown has a large recreational program that runs year-round. The town's sports complex offers tennis, soccer, basketball, volleyball, kickball, water sports, football and baseball. Mr. Tobarski is the coach of the indoor soccer team and as such spends a great many of his afternoons and weekends at the sports facility. Because of time-out options, late starts, inclement weather and so on, there are often children waiting for upwards of an hour for games to begin. These children are often without adult supervision and spend time running around, hanging out at the soda machine and generally being a nuisance. Mr. Tobarski would like to set up a reading area in the sports complex and talks with the Newtown School Department about such a facility.

The Superintendent of Schools feels that this is a great idea and is willing to fund some materials. The public library gets wind of the plan and offers assistance in the form of back issues of children's magazines and duplicate copies of books. The recreational department, recognizing its responsibility for supervising these waiting players and its liability in the event of accidents, agrees to hire a library-type person to supervise the room and the students. Since the majority of delays are on the weekends, the position is for ten hours per week, on Saturday and Sunday. The person will assist in selecting materials, maintain law and order in the room, keep the room orderly and so on.

The Newtown Elementary School has a fine library with Mr. Bernie Fischer in charge. Mr. Fischer feels that since most of the waiting players are students from his school—or graduates who have gone on to the middle or high school in town—he would be the perfect person for the job. He applies and is selected for the position. Mr. Fischer uses his time with these waiting players to provide assistance for their informational needs in school as well as a quiet place to relax while waiting to play or be picked up. Mr. Fischer begins to generate more interest among the waiting players for materials found in their respective school libraries. Ms. Lucinda Motte, the other elementary school librarian in town, feels that Mr. Fischer should not be generating more requests from students and should be keeping his part-time job quite separate from his full time-job at Newtown Elementary.

Questions:

1. Is what Mr. Fischer is doing on Saturdays and Sundays appropriate?

2. By providing a more personal assistance in the pursuit of information is Mr. Fischer clouding the waters between his two different responsibilities?

3. Is Mr. Fischer's Saturday and Sunday employment really a continuation of his full-time job?

4. What is Ms. Motte's role?

5. Should the Superintendent, the public library and the recreational department have thought through this project more clearly?

4. BIRTH, DEATH, INFINITY: BIBLIOTHERAPY

Todd, a second grader with acute leukemia, died last week. He had been in and out of school since the beginning of February and after the Easter vacation he was hospitalized. His mother was a very involved parent and often volunteered in his home room. The children knew that Todd was very sick and often talked with Todd and his mother about his illness. The classroom teacher, Harry Christopher, is new to teaching. He is very enthusiastic and is just devastated by the death of one of his students. He attended the funeral and has been in touch with the family. He has said nothing about Todd to his students. In fact, he removed Todd's desk and personal items early one Monday morning after Todd died and before the class came into the classroom.

James Singleton is the school library media specialist at Todd's school. He too knew the family. In fact, Todd's older sister often came in early to help Mr. Singleton get the library ready for the day's classes. Mr. Singleton has seen Todd's class in the library twice since Todd's death and feels that they are uneasy about what has happened. He also feels that they need to talk about Todd. The children have assigned seats in the library and Todd's is now unassigned. This late in the year it is unlikely that a new student will be placed in the Morris Elementary School. Mr. Singleton has asked Mr. Christopher about their talking jointly to the class about Todd's death. He has even recommended that together they read *The Fall of Freddie the Leaf* (Buscaglia, 1982) and discuss it. Mr. Christopher feels uneasy and says that since it is nearly Memorial Day, the children will soon be off for the summer and will forget about Todd.

Questions:

1. What should Mr. Singleton do?
2. Would a special exhibit of books on leukemia/death/recovery be inappropriate?

3. Since Mr. Singleton has contact with all students should he take the lead in this issue?

4. What should Mr. Christopher's role be?

5. Should Todd's mother be involved in talking with her son's former classmates and friends?

B. INFORMATION SERVICES

5. LIBRARY SERVICES TO TEACHERS IN GRADUATE SCHOOL

Misty Hatfield is a third grade teacher at the East Lawrenceville School. She is also getting a graduate degree in special education at Lawrenceville State University. This semester she is taking two classes at night, teaching full time during the day and planning her wedding. By her own admission, she is stretched to the limit and has little free time. Misty has to write a research report on the inclusion model in the elementary school. Because she has little time for research, she has asked Susanna Xiong, the school library media specialist at East Lawrenceville School, to check in some indexes and data bases for relevant information.

Unfortunately, the East Lawrenceville School serves a kindergarten through grade five population and does not have any specialized indexes or data bases. Susanna, ever the eager beaver, has asked one of her special library colleagues to check in commercial data bases and online systems for relevant information. One week later, a number of annotated searches arrive in the mail. Susanna gives them to Misty, secretly patting herself on the back for her efficiency. Misty extols her virtues during the teachers' meeting that afternoon. The next day Misty comes back to Susanna with her annotated list highlighted.

She now wants Susanna to obtain copies of the highlighted items on interlibrary loan. The East Lawrenceville School Library Media Center has no fax machine, no e-mail, and the phone is in the main office. For Susanna to get these items she will have to go to the local public or college library herself, determine who subscribes to what journals, use an ILL form to obtain the journals and try to get Misty to pay for any and all charges. What should she do?

Questions:

1. Should Susanna have offered these specialized bibliographic services in the first place?
2. What will happen if Susanna fails to deliver the articles?
3. What will happen if Susanna is able to deliver the articles?
4. Should the library media center have a policy on the type of support it offers to teachers for their graduate work?
5. How about a policy on the type of support offered to teachers who are researching and trying to change their curriculum?
6. Is there a difference?
7. Should there be?

6. TOO MANY STUDENTS, NOT ENOUGH BOOKS

Thomas Ankwomo has been the school library media specialist at Napier Elementary School for many years. He tries to assist the students with their research projects but often does not have enough materials to meet their needs. The school department gives the library only $3.00 per child per year for print materials; with an enrollment of 612 students, this is only $1836.00 for the library's annual book budget. Thomas makes his purchasing choices carefully and with full teacher input. He regularly maps parts of his collection, weeds, holds book fairs, writes grants and organizes a variety of other activities to keep his collection up-to-date in spite of the local funding problems. Unfortunately, because of the budget time frame, he is generally one year behind in his acquisitions.

This year, Thomas receives a request from the new sixth-grade teacher, Ms. Alves, for materials on twentieth-century presidents. Thomas pulls together individual biographies, searches collective biographies, finds encyclopedia articles, journal articles and chapters in nonfiction works on American history and government. Altogether Thomas collects 28 different sources and puts them on reserve for Ms. Alves' students. He offers to come into Ms. Alves' class to "book talk" each of these resources and to assist her in the classroom on a regular basis with this project.

While Ms. Alves is very happy with Mr. Ankwomo's work and welcomes him to her class, she teaches social studies to all five sixth grades—approximately 125 students. Ms. Alves wants each student to be able to pick a president and then borrow the materials on that president from the library. She would like the materials set aside on a separate shelf until each of her students has had the opportunity to select materials individually. Mr. Ankwomo feels that this is just not realistic given the size of the library's collection and the number of students that Ms. Alves teaches.

Questions:

1. What can Mr. Ankwomo do about this situation?

2. Should he try to convince Ms. Alves to keep the books on reserve in the library and allow the students to come in and work independently?

3. How about borrowing relevant materials on interlibrary loan from other school library media centers in the district, or from the public library?

4. If Mr. Ankwomo borrows materials on ILL, should he keep them on reserve or lend them out?

5. If borrowed materials are lost, who is responsible?

7. THE VERTICAL FILE—YES, NO, MAYBE

Tomas Castro has been teaching at The Brotherhood School for 30 years. He has kept newspaper clippings, pamphlets, government documents, association publications, maps and so on in a file in his classroom. These materials are now going to be sent to the library as Mr. Castro is retiring. The principal doesn't care what is done with them—he promised Tomas that they would go to the library and be appraised for tax purposes, but that's all. The new teacher in Tomas Castro's room just wants that "junk" out of the room and fast. Samuel Jackson, the school library media specialist at The Brotherhood School, knows that Tomas has kept his files in a general subject order. The files fill 12 file drawers, in three cabinets. Samuel, however, doesn't see the need for keeping these "clippings" as he calls them; he just wants the file cabinets. He tells Tomas that he will ask someone from the local library school to come over and appraise the collection for tax purposes and then make recommendations as to retention or disposal.

Patricia J. Sennett is a part-time instructor at the local university specializing in school library media centers. She comes over to The Brotherhood to examine Tomas Castro's files. Patricia feels that the files are a gold mine of historical information—the *Life* and *Look* magazines for November of 1963, the *Time* "Man of the Year" issues for 30 years; the local newspaper, clipped for anything about The Brotherhood School, along with copies of articles about graduates, immigrants, Vietnam, AIDs, Israel and the PLO. Local area publications are also included, such as those celebrating the rededication of the First Baptist Church, the welcoming parade for Gulf War Veterans, police and fire department brochures and miscellaneous publications of the local historical society. Patricia estimates the value of the file and recommends to Samuel Jackson that the files be reorganized along curricular lines or that a cross-reference system be developed to link what is in the files to existing courses. She feels that since all students study local and state history, the materials in Tomas Castro's files will fill a major gap in the collection. In addition, the major magazines such as *Time, Life* and *Look* present almost primary source material for specific time periods in American history. Background on students who have graduated and the impact of national issues such as AIDs, the PLO, Vietnam and the like on the local situation are next to impossible to find. The local newspaper is not indexed and the local public library only has back files on microfilm. Patricia makes her recommendations in writing and talks with Samuel about them. She offers assistance from some of her graduate students in organizing the files.

Samuel is most appreciative and writes to thank Patricia. He does not act on her recommendations but instead recruits parent volunteers to help him weed Tomas Castro's files from 12 drawers down to four. Six parents work on the collection and each is responsible for two drawers of the twelve.

Questions:

1. Should the files have been kept as originally given to the library?

2. Does Mr. Jackson have any responsibility to maintain and update this collection?

3. Of what value is a collection like this in an elementary school?

4. What would you do with the collection and regarding Dr. Sennett's recommendations?

5. Could part of the collection be sold off and the rest retained in a reorganized fashion?

8. TELEVISION AND LIBRARIES—LINKED?

The local cable company is required to produce a certain number of hours of local programming per month. Generally, this takes the form of political talk shows and round tables on local issues. Recently, Gerry Ramon, the school library media specialist for the Hopper Elementary School, was asked by a student to recommend a book on the life of Harriet Tubman. The child had just seen a network television show on the Underground Railroad. Gerry complied with the student's request but began to think about a new program.

That night, Gerry bought a local television guide for the coming week and marked off movies and specials in magic marker. Then he researched both his local public library and his elementary collection for titles that related to the network shows. He found lots of links. During February many of the networks showed films about Martin Luther King, the Civil Rights Movement, abolitionist activities during the Civil War, and so on. Gerry put together a tentative list of related materials and went to see the manager of his local cable station. Gerry proposed that at the beginning of each week, he prepare a short bibliography of materials related to shows to be broadcast during the coming week. The shows could be from networks, public television and commercial cable shows. Gerry would "booktalk" related works, perhaps tell a story, show the books and make bibliographies available in both the local elementary schools and the local public libraries.

The cable manager likes the idea and devotes 30 minutes on Tuesday evenings to Gerry's show. The show will be taped on Sunday. Gerry's plan is to get the local television guide each Friday after school and work on linking the TV material to books on Saturday. Through the Internet he can determine what library materials are available and prepare materials for his show as well as the printed bibliographies. He will photocopy the bibliographies on Monday morning and put them out for courier delivery throughout his local public library system and the other elementary schools.

Gerry becomes an overnight sensation within the local library world and soon is able to bring on some other library staff members to assist him in presenting his program. At the end of the school year, Gerry's principal mentions that he is concerned about Gerry's time on this project taking away from his responsibilities at school. Gerry points out that no work for the television show is done at school and in fact, by his being on the show, library circulation and requests for information have increased not only at Hopper but at all the other elementary schools in the district.

Questions:

1. Should Gerry abandon the school library media center for the world of television?

2. What is the principal's problem?

3. Is the concern valid?

4. Is preparing for the show not part of Gerry's responsibilities at Hopper?

5. Should the principal be asked to give Gerry time off to prepare for his show?

6. Where do the responsibilities for the school end and the commitment to the television show begin?

C. STUDY, SELECTION, AND EVALUATION OF REFERENCE MATERIALS

9. PICTURES IN THE PICTURE BOOKS

The first-grade class of the Fireside Elementary School was always eager to come to the library. Their teacher, Mr. Leese, worked closely with Ms. Ramirez, the school library media specialist, to present a program of story hours and related activities that were meaningful to the children. Together they worked on identifying and purchasing materials related to family and community, early school experiences and endangered animals.

As a result of their combined efforts, the library materials available to these children were second to none. This month the students have been studying families and have read a variety of books. Some have been read to them by Mr. Leese and others by Ms. Ramirez. About 12 have been checked out to be enjoyed independently in the classroom and now the class has come to the library to make individual recreational reading selections. As usual, Ms. Ramirez preselects about 100 titles, ranging across interest and reading levels and a variety of themes, using both fiction and nonfiction works. From these preselected works displayed around the primary reading area, the children are free to select any book. If a child has a particular title in mind which is not on display, he/she only has to ask for the book and Ms. Ramirez will secure it.

After all students have picked out a book to take to their class, they sing a song and exit the room.

The next morning in the middle of another class, Ms. Ramirez is interrupted by three little girls from Mr. Leese's room carrying the book *Tucking Mommy In* (Loh, 1988). Mr. Leese has written a note saying that this book is totally unacceptable. The children are full of conversation about the "dirty picture in the book." The class in the library is now all ears. Ms. Ramirez reads the note and is shown the "dirty picture" by the now giggling little girls from Mr. Leese's room. The picture shows a mother sitting on her bed, tired and not feeling well. She is in her slip and is in the process of removing it as her children help her into bed. Ms. Ramirez sends the girls back without the book or note but thanks them for bringing the book up to the room and gives them a special bookmark as a gift. She turns her attention to the class at hand.

At lunch time Ms. Ramirez seeks out Mr. Leese and talks with him. Following their conversation, Ms. Ramirez returns the book to the shelf in proper shelf order and considers the matter done with.

Two weeks later, Michaela, a student in Mr. Leese's room, asks Ms. Ramirez's help in finding "that book with the picture of the naked mommy."

Questions:

1. What was the substance of the conversation between Ms. Ramirez and Mr. Leese?

2. Was Ms. Ramirez correct in returning the book to the shelf without further comment?

3. Why did Ms. Ramirez put the book in its proper shelf place?

4. Did she want to bury it?

5. Should Mr. Leese have sent the book and note up with the children?

6. How should Ms. Ramirez answer Michaela's question?

10. ADD TO COLLECTION, SUBTRACT FROM COLLECTION

Mr. Richardson, the library media supervisor for the Capital Region School District, has been able to supplement his district's meager budget by buying books from remainder lists, from publisher overstocks and the like. He usually gets multiple copies of titles and passes them on to the school library media specialists throughout the district.

Recently, Mr. Richardson made a contact with the Health Supervisor for the district, who had money to spend for print materials on emerging health topics. Mr. Richardson was aware of a series of books called the Kids on the Block Series. The books deal with children facing health issues such as learning disabilities, physical handicaps and so on. Mr. Richardson purchased 35 copies of the entire series of books and forwarded them to the schools.

One week later, Mr. Richardson wrote to each of the school librarians and asked that the book *Friends for Life* (Aiello, 1988) be returned. His note indicated that the return was to be immediate and that under no circumstances was this book to be put on the shelf.

Friends for Life (Aiello, 1988) focuses on Amy Wilson, whose friend and teacher Natalie has AIDS.

Ms. Westin, one of the elementary school library media specialists in Capital Region, returns the book but presents herself at the end of the day in Mr. Richardson's office. Ms. Westin is 48 years old and has been a school library media specialist since 1968. She has worked in six school districts across the country, had glowing recommendations from each when she left to follow her husband, and has tangled with Mr. Richardson on a variety of issues. Ms. Westin is convinced that Mr. Richardson is censoring materials.

Questions:

1. What does Ms. Westin say to Mr. Richardson?
2. What is his response?
3. Why was the book pulled and in such a manner?
4. Does the Capital Region School District have a selection policy?
5. If yes, does this book fall within the selection guidelines?
6. Does it have a reconsideration policy?

7. Is this a censorship issue or simply one of heading off problems before they start?

8. What responsibility does the supervisor and the school library media specialist have regarding AIDS materials at the elementary level?

9. What about the health supervisor?

11. READ, READ, READ THEM ALL

The Lincoln School Department has a mostly suburban population base. The area is considered affluent and the library program (both public and in the schools) is well funded. Henrietta Place is the new middle school library media specialist. There is also a library media specialist at the high school and one at each of the four elementary schools.

Henrietta has had lots of middle school experience—as a teacher, a library aide and now as a library media specialist. She is also very aware of technology and very social. Henrietta meets the Superintendent of Schools from Lincoln at a dinner meeting one evening and again about three weeks later at another area dinner. During the second meeting, Henrietta makes quite an impression on the Superintendent and he asks to meet with her after the Christmas vacation.

About the middle of January, Henrietta gets a note asking her to drop by the Superintendent's Office the following Tuesday at 1 p.m. Henrietta meets with the Superintendent and the School Department's Business Manager. The subject: putting all of the elementary library collections online. Henrietta agrees to look at their collections and make recommendations. She is excused from her normal duties at the middle school for one week to complete this project.

Full of eagerness, Henrietta meets with the four elementary school library media specialists one Friday afternoon to lay out her game plan. They are most receptive but allude to a cataloging backlog at each of their libraries. From their conversation, Henrietta senses a significant backlog at each of the four schools and wonders why, since most books are bought with full processing and cataloging, and for the last year with MicroLif Data. The next Monday, Henrietta heads off to the first of the four schools to see the site, examine the collection and begin to put together a plan. What she sees on the shelf is an older collection, ill-suited to the students and to curricular needs. She sees that the collection itself is in good repair and the records (public catalog and shelf list) are up-to-date.

Only during lunch does the school library media specialist begin to talk about the collection. It appears that the woman has a locked closet full of books that are waiting for review. When Henrietta pursues this matter with her a whole story unfolds. It seems that since there is no supervisor for the library media specialists, these four people have banded together and agreed that they will each personally read every book purchased. Following that, they will discuss the books at one of their weekly Friday afternoon meetings, and only then will the books be placed on the shelf, the cards filed and so on. The school library media specialists feel that in the event of a challenge to one of their selections, they would be hung out to dry. Henrietta finds about 1500 titles in the closet, all in title order with the card sets inside. She is horrified but hides her concern.

Following through at the other three schools she finds much the same situation. All four have at least 1500 and maybe as many as 3000 current imprints waiting for reading and discussion. Since the library media specialists get together only once a week for about two hours and have many issues to discuss, the problem continues to grow in almost geometric proportions.

Henrietta does not write her report but rather, meets with the Superintendent and the School Department's Business Manager again. She informs them of the age of the collections on the shelf, unilaterally recommends not cataloging these older imprints and suggests that the Superintendent order the elementary library media specialists to get the books out of the closet and onto the shelves.

The Superintendent meets with the elementary library media specialists and discusses Henrietta's recommendations. They reiterate their concern that with no supervisor and no selection/ reconsideration policy, they stand alone in the event of a challenge. They emphasize that although they buy based upon review media, they cannot personally vouch for each book unless they have all read them. The Superintendent says he will think about the situation and get back to them.

Questions:

1. What would you do first?
2. Is there a role for Henrietta in the future with collection development, as library media supervisor or as the network manager?
3. Is the Superintendent out of line in expecting these school library media specialists to put books on the shelf without having personally read them?

12. SPECIAL COLLECTIONS IN THE ELEMENTARY SCHOOL LIBRARY MEDIA CENTER

James Nichols was a student at St. Maurice Elementary School for grades one through eight. Upon graduating from the regional high school, James opted for a career in the United States Army. While stationed overseas with a peace-keeping force, James was killed. The small suburban area where he grew up was shocked and wanted to establish a lasting memorial to the young soldier. After discussing it among themselves, James's family decided that establishing a specialized collection of materials at St. Maurice Elementary School would be a fitting tribute. Accordingly, donations were made to the school, which established a special collection in his memory and acknowledged the gifts. The family was informed of the names of the donors and a suitable plaque was engraved and hung in the entryway. The monies collected amounted to $8,000. In addition, several family members pledged to donate an annual amount of about $900 per year for the next ten years.

Sister Sarah Mary is the new librarian at St. Maurice. She never knew James but she knows of him and his family. It is her responsibility to select materials for the start-up of this collection and to maintain a wish list for future purchases from the annual monies. Sister Sarah Mary wants to purchase materials that will support the curriculum, but the family wants the materials to reflect James's reading interests—model building, stamp collecting and track and field. The family also wants materials on peace and war, death and dying. They want these items purchased so that they will be available for use by teachers and students faced with a similar tragic situation in their family. The Nichols family wants the materials housed in specially designed book cases which they will donate, and identified with special book plates. They want the items to be available for reference purposes only. Sister Sarah Mary is about to have her first meeting with the family where she will present them with a list of purchases she would like to make. She would also like to discuss their policies regarding circulation and housing of the collection.

Questions:

1. What should Sister Sarah Mary's strategy be?
2. What role should the family play in making decisions about reference vs. circulation?
3. What role should the family play in the question of specialized purchases in a narrow field vs. general curriculum support?
4. Is there a middle ground in this case?
5. Can some of the materials be purchased on divorce and other possible bibliotherapy areas?

6. How many track and field books or books on stamps or model building do you need?

7. Of what value are books on sports and hobbies if they cannot circulate?

8. Is there a role for this type of collection in an elementary school?

9. Will having this type of collection benefit the informational and recreational needs of the students and faculty at St. Maurice?

D. USER INSTRUCTION

13. CARD CATALOG VS. THE ONLINE CATALOG

For the last three years the Edmundton Elementary School has had an online catalog. The catalog consists of four networked IBM computers with two facilities for users' searches, one circulation station and one host machine. All records are in the system and new materials are purchased with machine-readable records. Mr. Kim, the school library media specialist, is considered by the other school library media specialists to be on the cutting edge of technology. Edmundton was the first of the elementary school library media centers to be computerized and Mr. Kim has spent long hours maintaining the integrity of the data base.

As part of his normal duties, Mr. Kim teaches regularly scheduled classes in library skills to students in grades three through five. He reviews alphabetical order, author, title and subject searching, arrangement of both fiction and nonfiction on the shelf—all using his card catalog. Mr. Kim does not feel that elementary school students are capable of understanding the online catalog and the search strategies involved in using it effectively. He has maintained his card catalog and his shelflist. He uses the online catalog for teacher searches and has taught the teachers how to use it.

Because of Mr. Kim's stature in the school library media community, the other school library media specialists are following his lead in maintaining both their online catalogs and their public card catalogs. They too hold off teaching the online catalog to students and use it to find student materials only after exhaustively searching the traditional card catalog. All feel that teaching online search skills to students is the domain of the middle schools.

Questions:

1. What makes Mr. Kim feel this way?
2. Is he correct?
3. Is he shortchanging his students?
4. How would you convince Mr. Kim to teach the online catalog?
5. Is it necessary to maintain both a card catalog and an online catalog after one full year of operation with an automated catalog?
6. At what point do you phase out a card catalog or eliminate it completely?

14. LIBRARY INSTRUCTION—FORMAL VS. INFORMAL

The principal of the Edmund School is required to observe untenured teachers three times during the first semester of each school year. The principal, Mr. Green, has been in the library to observe Ms. Grace twice. Each time the students were working diligently on activities related to the recently presented lesson on the card catalog. In addition, the students also were independently selecting materials and checking them out. The classes were orderly, quiet and on task. The students observed were in grades three and five. Today, Mr. Green observed Mrs. Grace with a first-grade class. In the first grade, students select a book and have a sharing time on one week (identified on Ms. Grace's schedule as Week A) and the next week, a story time and a related activity (identified on Ms. Grace's schedule as Week B). When Mr. Green told Ms. Grace that he would be observing her class during Week A when a first-grade class was in the room, Ms. Grace was quick to inform him that this was book week and little teaching, if any, would be taking place. Mr. Green explained that this was really just a formality and he would only be in the room for a brief time. He further indicated that he had seen quite enough in the two previous observations to prepare his report and that it would be a positive one.

Mr. Green came into the room when the first-grade students arrived and remained there for the whole teaching period. He wrote copiously during the entire time. During this class time the students began by singing several songs and reciting several poems that they had learned with Ms. Grace. Then they told her about the books they were returning or ones their classroom teacher had read to them during the week. Quietly, Ms. Grace called each table to the selection area to select a book to check out. The process was orderly and those waiting to be called or already finished with their selection sat at their assigned seats talking quietly. At dismissal, the principal told Ms. Grace that he was horrified that she would allow children to have a free period in which to talk.

Mr. Green has put his concerns in writing and wants Ms. Grace to have the children sit silently reading their library books and/or doing work sheets during book selection time. Mr. Green feels that allowing the children to talk during the book selection portion of the class is just not acceptable. He has further indicated to Ms. Grace that he will be back to observe this class in the future to see that his directions are being followed.

Questions:

1. What should Ms. Grace do?
2. Should she try to change the principal's attitude?
3. Should she try it his way?
4. Is little teaching taking place during the classes in B week?
5. Should Ms. Grace enlist the help of the classroom teachers in dealing with the principal?
6. When only a small portion of the class is out of their seats selecting materials should those at their seats sit silently or is quiet talking acceptable?

7. Should the entire class select at one time, say for 20 minutes?

8. Can Ms. Grace reach a compromise with the principal by preparing seat work related to recent books the students have read?

15. CD PRODUCTS—HEAVEN OR NOT?

Because of a school-wide budget initiative, the Mountainville Elementary School is the recipient of a major CD-ROM collection for its three Macintosh computers. Celia Mayorga, the library media specialist, has worked hard to secure this funding and has finally realized her dream. In addition to two general encyclopedias on CD, the library also has an animal encyclopedia, one on the United States Presidents, two different types of almanacs, and one atlas which also shows the country's flag, chief crops/products and plays the national anthem. Celia is in heaven. For younger students there are CDs of some popular children's stories such as Cinderella, Goldilocks and so on.

When school opens, Celia can't wait to show her colleagues and all the students in the building just what projects are possible with this new technology. Celia gives a brief overview to the faculty on the first day of school, showing a few of her tricks: the atlas playing the national anthem, and the animal encyclopedia focusing on facts and moving pictures demonstrating or illustrating them. For those teaching younger students or students just learning English, she has the CD say the word aloud as she points to an object on the screen. The word is said, the illustration shown and the spelling pops up in a window. The faculty are enchanted. Celia then follows up with a handout describing the new products. As her classes come to the library, she spends a great deal of time explaining the new products to the children, including some specifics on how they work and what they can be used for.

In virtually no time at all, Celia finds herself swamped with requests for information from the new CD-ROMs. The information, however, requires that the user sit at the work station, develop a search strategy and search for the required information. Complaining that they can't learn all this new techno-stuff just to get a map printed out or find some obscure fact on turtles, the faculty ask that Celia deliver the answers to their questions, not a strategy for finding the answers.

The first few times that a child arrives with a "quick question" printed on a piece of scrap paper, Celia complies. By the end of the first two weeks, word has spread that "Mrs. Mayorga will do it" and Celia finds herself overwhelmed and just a little confused. The library is a busy place but she seems to be doing other people's work. In addition, with only three CD-ROM search stations, not networked, there is a continuous line of children waiting to use the new tools.

Questions:

1. How did this situation arise?

2. What should/could Celia have done to avoid it in the first place?

3. What obligation does she have, if any, to move slowly with new technology and lay a proper foundation before showing "smoke and mirrors"?

4. What can Celia do now that people have discovered the CD-ROMs and their applications in the classroom?

5. What can Celia do to make her users realize that a commitment of time is necessary to learn how to use these tools effectively?

6. Do you agree that the user must learn to use the tools effectively?

7. Is it the role of the library media specialist to answer the question or to teach the user how to find the answer? Is there a difference?

16. ESL STUDENTS—CAN THEY LEARN CONTENT OR DO THEY JUST NEED SUPERVISION?

Mark Chen is an experienced elementary school librarian who has recently returned to his hometown of Urbanville to care for his aging parents. Mark is eagerly sought after by the local school library media supervisor to fill one of the many slots available at the Urbanville elementary schools. Mark selects the Rockway School and arrives during the last week of August to get things set up.

Rockway School's library media center is like many urban ones—a dated collection, a mishmash of furniture, a fixed schedule of classes, and so on. Mark has dealt with these challenges throughout his career and embarks eagerly to tackle the situation. He reviews the academic curricula which he's managed to get hold of, sets up a process to analyze the collection for gaps, hangs posters, sets up displays, arranges the shelves neatly, files some of the gigantic backlog of catalog cards, and generally gets things ready.

With the first day of school he finds that he has scheduled classes for "instruction in library skills" for grades three through five and storytime/book selection classes for grades one and two. There are three classes on his schedule, however, that are labeled "language arts supplement." Mark meets with the principal to find out more about these unfamiliar classes. What he finds out is that they are each classes of 25 non-English-speaking students. The principal explains that it would be a waste of time to teach these children about the library because they cannot understand enough English to use the library anyway. Further, he explains that Mark's responsibility to these "little kids" is to make sure they behave and do some dittos that come with their reader. Mark will be covering the classes while the teacher has her unassigned period. Mark appears puzzled but the principal assures him that there is no curriculum to follow with these kids; just have them work on their reading dittos.

The first two times Mark sees the kids, he realizes that their spoken English skills are not too bad but their reading skills are all over the ballpark. Some read at a beginning level, some are almost on grade level and some read not at all. Mark supervises the completion of their language arts dittos but is not happy about it. The children are well behaved but seem bored. Many want to get up and look at the books on display and some begin to read quietly to themselves or their neighbors while Mark helps others with their dittos.

At the first monthly meeting of school library media specialists, Mark seeks out some of his colleagues to find out what they do. It turns out that there is a common perception: that the language barrier prevents these ESL children from learning any of the content in the library media curriculum. All of the library media specialists either supervise ditto work or have a coloring period linked to a folk or fairy tale. Mark is determined to change this perception and make Rockway's program a model for the district.

Mark drafts some sample lessons on alphabetical order and the Dewey Decimal system and tries them out on the ESL children. They are enthusiastic and Mark makes an appointment to talk with the library media supervisor and his principal to lay out his plan for the delivery of a bona fide library media curriculum.

Questions:

1. Is the curriculum plan that Mark will present to his principal and the supervisor a watered down version? Is it really a second- or third-grade level massaged to look like fifth grade material?

2. What's wrong with supervising language arts work? Don't the children need more drill work in this area?

3. What is so important about the library content? Won't the children pick up library skills as their language improves and they work their way into a more traditional classroom?

4. How will Mark adapt (if that is his plan) the existing curriculum to these ESL students?

5. What special cultural and linguistic diversifications must Mark be aware of as he modifies the existing library curriculum?

6. Is it appropriate for Mark to take a proactive role in this situation?

II. Middle and Junior High School Library Media Centers

A. READERS' SERVICES

17. THE EARLY BIRD

The Gaylord Johnson Middle School is located in the heart of downtown Midland. This urban school has an enrollment of nearly 700 students in grades six through eight, along with several self-contained special education classes, some inclusion students and four self-contained English as a Second Language classes. Most of the children arrive by bus and thus there is very few after-school or before-school activities. Although the faculty generally arrive around 8 a.m., Mr. Amos, the Assistant Principal, is generally on duty from 7:30 when the first buses begin to arrive.

Miss Weston is the new library media specialist. Prior to moving to Midland, she was the librarian in a large urban high school in which teachers and students arrived in staggered shifts. Because of this, Miss Weston is used to arriving at work at 7 a.m. When she arrives, she is ready to work and begins to open the library early. Students who heretofore had to hang out in the front entry corridor until the bell rang at 8 o'clock feel that they have been given a sanctuary.

Because Miss Weston opens the library as soon as she arrives, by 7:45 she has generally circulated 40 or more books and answered a few brief reference questions. In addition, she has had a chance to get to know the students in a less formal, and often more supportive environment. While many students come in to get a book and leave, many stay on to browse, listen to their headsets, talk with friends, play cards and generally get ready to start the day in a relaxing environment. Some work in small groups on homework assignments and Miss Weston is often called upon to check answers or to assist. Miss Weston does not allow any foolishness and encourages respectful behavior.

One day, Mr. Amos walks by and realizes that there are about 60 students in the library. There is an organized type of chaos in the room as students prepare for the bell—books being checked out, reference books being shelved, pencils being sharpened and so on. He is visibly shaken by the sheer numbers of students present and asks Miss Weston what she is doing. Miss Weston says she's not sure but she plans on continuing. Mr. Amos brings in the Principal, Mrs. Roberts, who is equally surprised at the numbers of students. Miss Weston then shows them the circulation statistics for the last several weeks and they agree that something pretty terrific is happening.

Questions:

1. Miss Weston subscribes to several professional journals and hears about a grant for innovative library programs. Is this really a program?

2. Do extended hours and a place that is warm and fuzzy for urban middle school students require additional funding?

3. What would/could funding be used for?

4. Should Miss Weston be compensated for extending her hours?

5. How much recreation is going on vs. learning?

6. What, if anything, do the circulation statistics show?

18. CARTS IN THE CAFETERIA

The Northern Region Middle School Library Media Center has a fiction collection of about 1200 titles. Most are hardback, bought with long-forgotten federal monies. While clean and in good repair, they are obviously dated. Mrs. Corbitt, the Library Media Specialist, does not have a large budget and feels that the lion's share of her funds should go to support the curriculum and not recreational reading. The fiction that she does purchase in hard copy is generally award-winning and often requested for a particular language arts or social studies class. She almost never buys paperbacks.

Recently, the local Chamber of Commerce offered grants of up to $1500 to schools and school library media centers for innovative programs. Mrs. Corbitt decides to apply and use her money to support a paperback collection.

After discussing the project with her supervisor and her building level principal, Mrs. Corbitt requests funding for a "Carts in the Cafeteria Exchange Program." Modeled after some of the interesting carts she has seen in the malls around town, this cart would be a colorful and large (but not unwieldy) book truck. Books (preferably paperbacks) would be donated by area merchants, parents, teachers and students. The whole school community would be encouraged to donate their used but not abused books for the cart. During the breakfast and lunch periods, on two rotating days during the week, the members of the student council would wheel out the cart and students who were interested in reading a paperback or just looking at the offerings would be able to browse and exchange. While the program is an exchange one, Mrs. Corbitt feels that no student should be denied a book from the cart just because he or she hasn't brought one in. Mrs. Corbitt realizes after she spells out the program that the only money she needs is for the cart. She sends in her request for $325.00.

Questions:

1. Is providing for recreational reading needs of the students the job of the school library media center?

2. Is Mrs. Corbitt right in only buying fiction that is award-winning and curriculum-related?

3. What about the hardback copy only policy?

4. Can the Carts Program be expanded to buy materials and set up some kind of paperback library?

5. Will having the fiction on an exchange cart meet the readers' needs for recreational and interesting/relevant fiction?

19. THE LOUNGE FURNITURE VS. THE TABLES AND CHAIRS

Mr. Pena is the library media specialist at the Newton Township Junior High School. Newton Township is a suburban area that is primarily a bedroom community situated between aging cities. The students at Newton Township are upwardly mobile and very achievement oriented. Most of the graduates finish high school and 72% go on to a four-year college. Students are heterogeneously grouped for all classes but because of the nature of the total school population, there is not much of a spread in abilities or commitment to work.

Teachers at Newton Township, including Mr. Pena, have been in the building for several years and rarely transfer out. The school has a warm and caring environment.

The library media center is located on the first floor of the three-story building. The building was built in the 1960s and while not crowded, is certainly full. There is a complete flexible schedule and enough space in the room to accommodate large groups for instruction and small groups or individuals working unsupervised.

Over the summer Mr. Pena cleaned out his parents' house when they moved into a smaller apartment. While much of the furniture was given away, Mr. Pena kept a love seat, a three-cushioned couch and two large wooden rocking chairs. He also kept a few side tables and a large coffee table with a three-door compartment. He decided to "revamp" the library image and brought all of the pieces into his school.

Upon entering the library media center the user was in front of the circulation desk. To the right were tables and chairs for 30 students. To the left were small tables with three or four chairs per table. Total seating in that part of the room was about 20. Mr. Pena removed two tables and six chairs that had been on the left side of the room. He replaced them with the couch. Next to the couch he placed one of the end tables and in front of the couch he placed the coffee table. On the other side of the coffee table, Mr. Pena placed the two rockers. He put another side table between them. On each of the side tables, Mr. Pena placed some new library books and on the coffee table he placed a globe and the daily newspaper.

Mr. Pena had his own desk near the circulation desk, on the left side of the room. He never sat there, generally preferring to sit at one of the tables or at the circulation work station. His drawers in the desk were empty, as he kept most things in his file cabinet. Mr. Pena removed his desk from the library media center and put the love seat in its place. As he looked around, he was able to spread things out more and realized that by removing the two tables and six chairs and adding in the furniture from his parents' house he could seat one more person, perhaps two. He also gave the illusion of more openness to the room.

The first day of school, the principal walks in and is extremely alarmed. He wonders what kind of services will be provided to readers in a lounge environment. He feels that the students do not come to the library to relax but to learn. He doesn't feel that the materials will be used as they were designed to be in this type of setting. He reiterates to Mr. Pena that Newton Township students are achievers and readers and learners. He feels that this new image of the library media center is not consistent with the message that the school wants to deliver to students and their parents.

Questions:

1. What should Mr. Pena do?

2. How does the concept of the library as a gathering place vs. the library as a place for peace and quiet study fit in here?

3. Will this new environment encourage more use of the collection or more foolishness?

4. Should Mr. Pena have discussed with the principal his idea for revamping the library space?

5. How will the couches and chairs be maintained? What will happen as they wear out? Will parents be encouraged to donate their used furniture?

6. What type of image do couches and rockers project to the serious learner?

7. Is the room more inviting this way or was the more traditional appearance what readers expect?

8. Does Mr. Pena have an obligation to provide a welcoming environment to encourage the use of his collection?

9. Will the new furniture encourage parents to come in and use the room? How about community groups?

10. Are parents and other adults to be encouraged in this direction? Is the library media center the hospitality suite of the school?

11. Does the hospitality suite have an obligation as a library?

20. MEET THE AUTHOR

Each year at Brown Avenue Middle School, the Parent Teacher Organization provides funds for a Visiting Author program. The PTO pays for the honorarium and for light refreshments during the book signing. Typically the day takes on the format of two large group assemblies in the morning and then one group of about fifty students selected from across grade levels to work with the author on some part of process writing. This one-hour working session is followed by the book signing and reception. The library media specialist handles all of the details and uses her book fair money to provide housing for the author's one night in town, meals for that time period, and to buy duplicate copies of the author's books prior to his or her arrival so that the children will be knowledgeable about them. In addition, the library is closed for business on the day of the visit and the school department sends a substitute to help out. This is truly a joint effort on the part of the school and the parents.

This year, the PTO has been replaced by the Site Team Committee. This Committee is made up of six teachers elected by the faculty and five parents elected by the parents at the first open house of the year. The principal also serves on the Site Team Committee but does not chair it. The chair rotates among the Team members on a monthly basis. This month, the chair is a parent and the topic is the budget for programs like the Author Visit.

Vanthy Ho is the library media specialist at Brown Avenue. She has been there for the last nine years and instituted the visitation program. This year she has arranged for a very prolific author to visit. The woman has been a Newbery Honor writer three times in the last ten years and writes about young adults in a realistic fashion. Her works are well regarded but under-represented in the collection. Ms. Ho needs to add many titles, in duplicate copies, to the collection prior to the author visit. The visit is scheduled for May and it is now October. She is assured of the money for the honorarium but will need more to buy the books. In addition, many of this author's works are available on audio-tapes and one of her books has been made into a television movie. Ms. Ho needs to acquire these in multiple copies as well.

As Ms. Ho prepares her presentation before the Site Team, she becomes discouraged. She questions whether or not paying for additional copies and copies in an audio-visual format is the right way to go. She wants to provide materials in a variety of formats but has never had to go the AV route before. She wonders if the parents will see her side of the issue.

Questions:

1. Is Ms. Ho right to wonder about parent support?

2. If the program has been viable all these years, should she be concerned?

3. How should her presentation proceed?

4. Is providing books by the author in multiple copies and various formats going to stimulate some of the less than enthusiastic readers to try to become familiar with the visitor's works?

5. She's never prepared bibliographies of the works of the visitors before. Should she now? If she does, should they be annotated and indicate various formats?

6. How should she deal with the student who wants to borrow the film or audio tape but not the book?

B. INFORMATION SERVICES

21. PATRON INFORMATION

Patricia Calhoun is a new English teacher at St. Peter's Academy. The school, located about five miles outside of Middlevale, enrolls about 1000 day students in grades six through twelve. Patricia teaches in the lower school, grades six through eight.

Patricia is up for tenure this year and is very nervous. Her background in her subject is strong and she works very hard. Her biggest problem is motivating her students. She tends to lecture in her classes and only occasionally has cooperative group work or projects that require a thematic approach.

This year Patricia has asked the library media specialist, Rosario Amato, to help her prepare a reading list for her seventh-grade classes. She has decided that each student will do one book project per quarter and she has a host of choices of project types, many of them very creative. Together she and Rosario go through the collection and come up with about 100 titles. Many are titles with which Patricia is unfamiliar but she relies on Rosario's endorsement as she makes her choices. Rosario uses her online scanner to print out an annotated bibliography as well as a title list of books for Patricia. She keeps a copy at the circulation desk and another copy at the area reserved for Patricia's books.

Several weeks go by. Some of Patricia's books have circulated and been returned, others are still out. Rosario has a sense that the project is well underway. Some students have told her that they like the selection and are buying the books in paperback at the mall. Patricia stops by every few days to look at what is on the shelf. One morning, she comes over to Rosario and asks her to give her a list from the computer of titles that have circulated and to whom. She would also like another list giving the names of the students and the books they've taken out. Rosario looks at her and says: . . .

Questions:

1. What would you say?
2. Is this a legitimate service?
3. Assuming that the library's online system can generate such a list, is this something that Rosario is free to make available?
4. Are there legal issues involved here? How about patron privacy?
5. Rosario has followed every known acceptable behavior in working with the teacher and in providing assistance to the class. Is this a "reference" transaction? How does this differ from what Rosario has already done for Patricia?
6. Rosario provides circulation statistics every month to the principal; what's so different about this?
7. Can Rosario comply with part of Patricia's request?
8. Can she modify the request and provide some general data?
9. Why is Patricia seeking this information from Rosario instead of from the students themselves?

22. INTERLIBRARY LOAN

Veronica Gellen is the librarian at the Hopewell Middle School. The school is new, only three years old, and the collection is relatively up-to-date. There is an online catalog and several CD products.

Veronica has had a great deal of difficulty with her principal, who is a traditionalist. The principal wants Veronica to hold skills classes for all of the grade levels. Veronica wants to have a completely flexible schedule. They reach a compromise and Veronica gets a fixed schedule for the sixth grades and an open or flexible schedule for the seventh and eighth grades. Veronica is determined to show the principal that this open or flexible schedule is the way to go. She works on developing a unit with the seventh grade science teachers on the subject of famous inventors and mathematicians. They compile a list of famous people that the students will research. They develop a time frame for the project and criteria for grading it. Because the library is adjacent to a large Macintosh Computer Lab, they decide that the students will be required to type their projects.

The planning for the project has been in the works since the first week of school. The project will begin on the first day after Columbus Day. It is now October 1st and Veronica decides to begin to identify appropriate resources in her collection. It is her intention to put them on reserve so that the students will be able to get to the biographical documentation quickly, and not waste time trying to find the resources on the shelf and in the online catalog. Veronica checks the online catalog, the various specialized and general encyclopedias, the CD products and the collected biographies. Alas, the collection at Hopewell comes up very short. There are about 45 names of mathematicians and inventors from the earliest times to the present. Students must find biographical information along with career or discovery information. Where possible they are to provide examples of the biographee's work and a picture. Beyond a few of the more famous who are in the encyclopedia or in one or two books on famous mathematicians or giants of invention, the collection just can't support this project. Veronica calls the librarians at the six other middle schools in the district and asks if they will help her.

Questions:

1. What would you say if you received an SOS from Veronica?
2. Why did Veronica let the project get this far without checking her resources?
3. Is Veronica right in pulling the sources so that the students

don't have to "waste time finding the resources on the shelf or in the online catalog?"

4. Will Veronica's lack of resources give the principal more ammunition to give her fixed classes?

5. Is there a role here for public library cooperation?

23. THE EAGER RABBIT

Marion Shea is the new library media specialist at the Nationburg Middle School. She has been a school library media specialist for many years but has only recently relocated and found herself at Nationburg. The collection there is pretty dismal, there is a virus in the online catalog and teachers have little or no faith in the library media center. Marion works from dawn to dusk and by the end of six weeks the physical space looks great and there is no longer a virus in the online system. Some seventh- and eighth-grade teachers are even venturing in for projects, and Marion pulls out all the stops. She is available to do whatever, whenever.

Richard Henry is a sixth-grade language arts teacher. He is polite when he sees Marion in the corridor but he never comes to the library. Marion sends him a note after her first month at Nationburg, inviting him and his students into the library media center. Richard ignores the note and his students don't come to the library. Finally, Marion takes the bull by the horns and seeks Richard out one morning before school. Richard tells her that he has a project well underway and because of the nature of the library media center over the past few years, has found a way to work with the public library. He is impressed by Marion's enthusiasm and promises that the next project will involve her and the Nationburg library media center. Marion is placated.

Several weeks later, Marion is in the local branch of the Nationburg Public Library. She happens to see Penny, the children's librarian, hard at work and stops by to see what she's doing. Penny explains that Richard is a good friend and that she is trying to round up enough copies of the Kerr book, *When Hitler Stole Pink Rabbit* (Kerr, 1987), for Richard's students to read as a class. She is under the gun to find 20 copies within the week. Marion wishes her well and heads off to find her own items.

Marion decides that this is her golden opportunity to prove her worth and that of the Nationburg library media center to Richard. She looks in the online catalog for the book by Kerr, then drives around to all of the branches and checks out all copies on the school library card. On Monday morning she calls the librarians at several of the district's elementary schools and asks them to send her as many copies as they can spare. By Thursday, Marion has 22 copies and sends a note to Richard telling him that she "heard" from Penny that he was looking for a classroom set of the books. Richard is thrilled.

Questions:

1. Do Marion's actions follow the accepted definition of "information services?"

2. Hasn't Marion provided personal assistance to library users in pursuit of information?

3. Marion has made a convert of Richard. Isn't this OK?

4. The students have all received a copy of the novel to read. What, if anything, did Marion do wrong?

5. Should Marion have told Penny she would take care of getting Richard his copies?

6. Did Richard err in not informing Marion of his new project?

7. How could Marion have resolved this situation without making Penny look as though she couldn't deliver, and without resorting to these type of tactics herself?

8. What strategies can you suggest for Richard and Marion and Penny to work together for the future?

9. Has long-term damage been done to any of the parties?

24. HIGH INTEREST AND LOW READABILITY VS. LOW READABILITY

Lucinda Klee is the reading teacher at Hill Hollow Junior High School. She has the responsibility for going into the academic classrooms three days a week in support of reading in the content area for the seventh grade. The other two days, Lucinda sees those same students for reading in a self-contained environment. The students range in abilities from non-reading ESL students to those reading on a high third-grade level. While some of the students have clearly defined reading difficulties, many receive reading instruction because their English language proficiency is not on grade level.

The school department has provided Lucinda with a basal reader for students up to a reading level of eighth grade. They have provided her with black-lined masters, supplementary lists and so on. It is her responsibility to raise the reading levels of each of her charges by a significant amount by the year's end.

Lucinda realizes that the basal reader is just not meeting the needs of these seventh graders who happen to be reading on a third grade level or below. She decides to use trade books in the classroom for those days when the students are self-contained for reading. She discusses her idea with her counterpart in the eighth grade and they agree to identify about six titles for each reading level. They agree not to overlap.

Lucinda comes into the library media center with her list of titles for her seventh graders. There are two for which she is looking for backup materials: *The One in the Middle Is the Green Kangaroo* (Blume, 1992) and *Henry and Mudge and the Careful Cousins* (Rylant, 1994). The other titles are similar in nature but Lucinda already has identified support materials for them. Grace Hernandez is the library media specialist who is on duty when Lucinda arrives. Grace has been an elementary school library media specialist for the last several years in an elementary school in Hill

Hollow. She is very familiar with the trade book emphasis in the elementary grades and is delighted that Lucinda is exploring options beyond the basal. She is quite shocked to find that these second grade titles are being proposed for middle school students. What should Grace do?

Questions:

1. Define backup materials.
2. Is Lucinda making the trade book titles into basal readers?
3. If so, does Grace have any obligation to step into this situation?
4. Does Grace have an obligation to point out that giving obviously elementary titles to middle school students is not age- or interest-appropriate?
5. Can Grace come up with a counter list of high-interest, low-readability titles?
6. Are these titles that are available in the library media center?
7. What are her options if they are not readily available?
8. Is this an appropriate use of Grace's time?

C. STUDY, SELECTION AND EVALUATION OF REFERENCE MATERIALS

25. GIFT HORSES

Each year Marilyn Tomas, the library media specialist at the Holiday Hills Middle School, travels to Washington, DC to visit her sister. The trip is always made in the summer, during the school vacation, and is not complete without a trip to the Gifts and Exchange Division of the Library of Congress. As a representative of her school, Marilyn may select duplicates being discarded by the Copyright Office. Marilyn spends many happy hours selecting materials, arranged willy-nilly on shelves. She knows that her school could never afford the quantity and quality of items she finds here. Marilyn has an arrangement with her principal whereby, on her own time, she spends hours at the Library of Congress and the principal pays to ship any library materials back to the school library media center.

This year, there was a large amount of young adult fiction to select from. Much of it was familiar to Marilyn from her reading of professional journals and various review media. Some of it she selected quickly based upon the reputation of the author and/or the publisher. She was quick to avoid presses that were religious in orientation and things that she remembered as being poorly reviewed. Because of the severe time constraints at the Library of Congress, Marilyn always selected more than she might use at her middle school, farming books out to the public and high school libraries in her area.

When September dawned and Marilyn was back at Holiday Hills, she found that she had selected a large quantity of fiction, far too much for her to catalog and process with complete bibliographic records. Through the auspices of the Parent Teacher Organization, the cataloging of these items was paid for by the sale of candy and ice cream. Marilyn simply had to send off a list of authors, titles and ISBN numbers to get complete MicroLif records to add to her system. Because of the time delay in receiving MicroLif records, Marilyn often quickly processes the books, especially fiction, and puts them out on the shelf for circulation. Upon receipt of the MicroLif data disk, Marilyn completes the processing of the item.

Patrice Jackson is a seventh grader at Holiday Hills. Patrice is a special needs student who is mainstreamed for all of her academic classes and receives support services from a Special Education Teacher on a "pull out" basis. Today, Patrice finished her work with the resource teacher and asked for a pass to come to the library. Marilyn was just putting out the new fiction from the Library of Congress when Patrice arrived. Patrice selected not one but two of the titles and checked them out.

The next day, Patrice sought out Marilyn to tell her that she was returning one of the books she had taken because it had "nasty things" in it. Patrice said that she showed the book to her mother and Mrs. Jackson was very upset about what her daughter was reading. Patrice indicated that Mrs. Jackson would be calling Marilyn that afternoon to find out why the library owned such an item.

Patrice was very anxious to show Marilyn the offending parts and then returned to her class. Marilyn read the section that Patrice had shown her and had to agree that the phrase was sexually explicit. Just then, the telephone rang.

Questions:

1. Do gift books such as these come under the library's Book Selection Policy?

2. If there is such a policy and it follows the general American Library Association guidelines, what recourse does Marilyn have? What about Mrs. Jackson?

3. What is the first thing that Marilyn should say to Mrs. Jackson?

4. Does Marilyn have an obligation to read or find reviews for everything she puts into the collection?

5. Is this possible, given that Marilyn added 300 new titles to her collection from her summer jaunt to the Library of Congress?

6. Why is Marilyn quick to avoid selecting materials that come from religious publishers? Does she not have an obligation to make all types of materials available? By doing this is she not practicing censorship?

26. NOT THE BABY-SITTERS CLUB

Mr. Alvarez is a single parent, trying to raise his twin boys, Edwin and Jose. Both boys receive help in school for ADD (Attention Deficit Disorder). Mr. Alvarez works hard to maintain a structured time frame at home so that the boys' school work is done before any television is watched or computer games are played. The boys receive a weekly allowance from which they may make small purchases. They also receive larger amounts of money when they do something special—weed the garden, shovel snow, and so on.

Jose has about $12.00 which he has been saving to spend at the school book fair. He knows that he can purchase about four books and perhaps some pencils and erasers, maybe even a book cover. The first day of the book fair, Jose finds a package containing a small flashlight and a copy of *Scary Stories to Tell in the Dark* (Schwartz, 1986). He is intrigued by the idea of reading late at night with the flashlight but unfortunately, the package costs $12.50. He thinks he will ask Edwin to lend him the extra fifty cents. While browsing in the other shelves, however, Jose finds a number of the new books by R. L. Stine. The series is called *Baby-Sitter* and the covers are intriguing and gruesome. While standing there, Jose realizes that he can buy all three of the titles in this series for the twelve dollars that he has. The decision is made—Jose purchases one copy of each of the *Baby-Sitter* volumes that are for sale. Because the parent volunteer knows Jose, when she rings up his purchase she gives him one of the promotional brochures that the publisher has provided for this series.

That evening, following the completion of his homework, Jose gets his books and the poster out from his backpack to show his father. He explains about the night light and the cost, and continues to extol his "great deal" with his twelve dollars and the acquisition of these three titles. He tells about getting the poster from Mrs. MacGregor, the parent volunteer manning the book fair. Mr. Alvarez is not pleased. He finds the covers too gruesome for his seventh grade son and worries that the books will promote violence. He finds the picture of the baby-sitter too enticing for his young sons. His sons are often with a baby-sitter after school and he is concerned that the reading of these books will spark some foolish behavior on their part.

Questions:

1. Book fairs are one way to raise money for school library media centers and this one was no exception. What obligation does the library media specialist have to help children select age/interest appropriate items to purchase?

2. How can Mr. Alvarez handle this situation with his sons? Should he drop the matter? Read all five books and go to see the principal? Demand his money back?

3. What about the matter of the poster? It was free and no one forced Jose to take it. Did the parent volunteer have any responsibility to suggest that these books may be too violent for a seventh grader or that the poster was too explicit?

4. Should the criteria for books, posters and the like that are sold at the book fair fall under the same guidelines as items acquired for the library media center? In other words, does the book selection policy apply here?

27. ETHNIC AND CULTURAL SENSITIVITY

Rose Littleton is a science teacher at the eighth-grade level at the Henderson Middle School. She has been teaching there for about five years and before that worked in a medical research lab. Rose loves her students and they love her. She is friendly with them but still earns their respect.

Rose is a Native American and very involved in tribal activities in the New England area. She and her family travel to powwows and gatherings throughout the region. Rose is one of the few minority teachers at Henderson.

The library media center at Henderson is staffed by Mrs. Toliver. Mrs. Toliver has earned the respect of her students and the faculty for her hard work in building and maintaining the collection. She is able to secure grants to provide for innovative programs and to arrange for outside speakers on topics of interest to the students, and is always available to provide resources to the school community.

One of the ideas that Mrs. Toliver has for the coming school year is to have the students nominate and vote on their favorite work of fiction. The guidelines are still being developed by the language arts faculty but in general any student may nominate any book during a one-week period. All books nominated will be put on a special shelf in the library. A grant has been secured to provide duplicate copies as necessary. Over a 30-day period, the books will be read by the students and voted upon. To vote, a student must read at least three of the nominated titles.

The nominated titles list has just come out. As one might imagine, they range from Newbery winners to pulp-type works. Mrs. Toliver sets about securing duplicates, running off forms for evaluation and publishing a list of the nominees and the rules. Rose Littleton gets the nomination list in her mailbox and is furious to see that one of the titles nominated is *The Indian in the Cupboard* (Banks, 1981). Rose heads straight to the library and demands that the title be removed from the contest. Mrs. Toliver informs Rose that the book was nominated by many students and it is too late to stop the contest or withdraw the book. Rose says that just because a title is popular doesn't mean it is appropriate. She feels that the book demeans her people by its stereotypical portrayal of the Indian. She tells Mrs. Toliver that she is off to see the principal.

Questions:

1. Does Rose Littleton have the right to interfere with a library media center promotional idea?

2. Does the contest have to follow the same guidelines as those in the book selection policy?

3. Is Mrs. Toliver under any obligation to defend herself or ignore the matter?

4. What do you think the principal will do? Should do?

5. Should Rose have been involved in this contest earlier on, and perhaps been given a copy of this list of nominated books so that she could see if any were insensitive to ethnic issues? Is this a type of censorship?

6. Should Mrs. Toliver have had a committee of ethnic and cultural representatives to assist her with this contest and perhaps develop rules for nominated books?

7. Is this much ado about nothing?

28. EASY READING SELECTION

The East Hopkinton Junior High School has an enrollment of about 900 students in grades seven through nine. Many of the children are reading significantly below grade level and the school has a large Chapter One program. In addition, there is a disproportionate number of children receiving free lunch and breakfast, compared with other junior high schools in the city. The school population at East Hopkinton has shifted over the last five years from a solid middle-class environment to one with high student mobility, lots of disadvantaged students, and an abundance of English as a Second Language and Bilingual students.

The library media center at East Hopkinton continues to be the curriculum center of the school. The collection is well used by all members of the school community. The librarian, Mr. Rivero, works hard to keep the collection current and attractive. He meets regularly with the principal and the other members of the faculty to keep abreast of curricular changes.

While his circulation figures are high, Mr. Rivero doesn't feel that the students are actually reading the books. He has noticed that many of the books in his fiction collection seem to circulate on the basis of their covers. Often the children borrowing the books cannot read even the title aloud to him when he's checking out the book to them. When he tries to steer them to books with fewer words and more pictures they appear confused.

After talking with some of the faculty, Mr. Rivero makes an appointment to see Dr. Stein, the a professor of reading over at the local university. Dr. Stein teaches many courses in content area reading and children's literature. He has run several in-service programs for East Hopkinton and that's where he and Mr. Rivero first met. After talking with Dr. Stein, Mr. Rivero has a plan of attack.

Over the next few weeks new titles are added to the collection and some are removed. Picture books or those that give the appearance of being picture books (oversized, heavily illustrated, and Caldecott winners or honor books) are removed and sent to one of the elementary schools in the district. New high-interest, low-readability titles are added in paperback, as are illustrated versions of classics. Books in the collection for which a video has been made are cross-referenced so that a child who borrows *The Whipping Boy* (Fleischman, 1986) knows that there is also a film that has been made from the book. While the film is not in the collection, a list of local video stores is available.

The circulation continues at about the same level as before but now children often come in with their friends and what one returns, the other borrows. Mr. Rivero feels that the children really are reading. The faculty and administration of the building go along with Mr. Rivero because of his commitment to the children and the program, but there are the beginnings of discontent with the illustrated versions of classics and the link between the books and videos.

Questions:

1. What's going to happen next?

2. What can Mr. Rivero do to keep his circulation high and meet the reading needs (primarily at this point recreational) of his new English readers?

3. The collection policy is vague on illustrated or comic versions of books, and after all the library does have the "real" version. Should the policy be more specific?

4. Is Mr. Rivero correct in believing that the books are circulating but not being read? How would he confirm or deny this?

5. Is there a problem linking literature and videos? Won't the child borrow the book but not read it and watch the video instead?

D. USER INSTRUCTION

29. THEMATIC UNITS

Xiomarah Perez is the Library Media Specialist at the Covenant Middle School. The school has spent a great deal of money this year putting the teachers into academic teams (English, math, social studies and science). Extensive in-service was provided and continues as the year progresses. The students are assigned heterogeneously to a team, and will stay with these same four teachers for the duration of their middle school years. Xiomarah sees the students in a fixed class schedule upon their entrance to Covenant—at sixth grade. She teaches them how to use the online catalog, the *Childrens's Magazine Guide,* and reviews the almanac, atlas, encyclopedia and dictionary. The students only come to the library for one semester, but twice weekly during that time.

As a special subject teacher, Xiomarah was not included in this special in-service program but she supports the concept. Xiomarah approaches the Sixth-Grade Team (they call themselves the Pegasus Program) and asks about integrated units they will be teaching. They tell her that for the first part of the year they will be focusing on ancient cultures, primarily Greece, Rome and Egypt. They have fully integrated social studies and English for this time period and are working on science and math. Xiomarah tells them she will use Egypt as her theme for sixth grade and teach the traditional library media skills through this theme.

Xiomarah scours the literature for thematic units that have been done and finds some, but they are not on ancient civilizations. She decides to develop her own. She begins by looking for a book in the library that will serve as an anchor, and finally settles on the book by David Macaulay called *Pyramid* (Macaulay, 1975). She borrows the video from the district's library and shows it to introduce her unit. As she moves on to the teaching of the online catalog, she uses examples involving the subject of Egypt. She does the same for keyword searching and for author and title. The children seem interested. She does the same for the *Children's Magazine Guide,* and when she does the dictionary the children develop their own Egyptian dictionary.

As the semester ends and Xiomarah prepares for the next group from the Pegasus Program, she wonders if she hasn't artificially developed a program that really doesn't stick. She has not done much with themes and is unsure that this is the way to go.

Questions:

1. Will developing thematic units teach users about library services and tools or will it teach them more about the theme — in this case, Egypt?

2. If Xiomarah teaches skills through the theme of Egypt for the first semester, what should she do for the second? Presumably the Pegasus Program has moved on to another topic in social studies by this time.

3. If Xiomarah has a curriculum, how can she meet its demands by teaching to or through a theme?

4. Shouldn't Xiomarah insist upon in-service like the other teachers before she embarks on this type of venture?

5. Without in-service or training, might Xiomarah do more harm than good?

6. In a thematic unit, what is the point or purpose of an anchor book?

7. Did Xiomarah set a poor tone by showing a video to start off the unit?

30. THE STYLE MANUAL

The Penn Middle School enrolls about 700 students in grades six through eight. The students come from a variety of elementary schools in the district. As a result of their varied elementary school backgrounds, the students' reading and writing skills are equally varied.

Naomi Segal, the head of the English Department at Penn, is very concerned about writing. She has each of the six members of her department have their students write a composition each week along with regular book reports, short stories and two research papers per year. The sixth-grade teachers establish the tone for the research paper because almost no sixth grader has ever done one before. The sixth-grade teachers work very hard on note taking, outlining, bibliography format, footnotes and so on. When the students get to seventh grade the process is repeated but confusion ensues because there is no single style for footnotes and bibliography accepted by all of the teachers.

Naomi has her hands full with the concerns of the department and the six members of the department have their hands full with their classes. They meet weekly, and early in September decide to approach the principal with this dilemma. They want someone to assume responsibility for developing a style manual for the school, and perhaps for the district. The principal decides that bibliography is the responsibility of the library media specialist and enlists his help.

Mark Cabot is the library media specialist at Penn. He sees the sixth-grade in a fixed schedule and the seventh and eighth grades in a flexible environment. Mark meets with the principal and with Naomi. He welcomes the responsibility for developing a style manual and goes so far as to say he will arrange to meet with the other middle school library media specialists in the district and with those in the high school. He feels that a single style manual for the district, to be used beginning in grade six, is the way to go.

Mark calls several of the library media specialists in other districts and asks them what they do. A few have established style manuals and send Mark copies. Mark arranges to meet with his own English teachers and get some parameters from them. His plan is then to draft a manual and present it to the teachers in his building. From there, he will follow it through the other middle and high schools in the district.

Questions:

1. Is this type of project an appropriate use of the library media specialist's time?

2. Why doesn't the English department take on this responsibility?

3. Can the English Department work cooperatively with the district's library media specialists on this project?

4. Does this type of task or responsibility fall under the term "user instruction?"

5. Is Mark going to then teach the style manual to his sixth graders, or at least introduce the concept of footnote and bibliography form?

6. Will Mark then get involved in teaching this to his seventh and eighth graders when they come to the library?

7. Is this the purpose of the library media center and the specialist—to teach bibliographic format?

8. By preparing this manual, and with such enthusiasm, does Mark set a tone for handling other projects that someone feels is the responsibility of the library media center?

31. NEW USERS AND THEIR PROJECTS

Melinda Ferrante is a math teacher at the Heritage Junior High School. She has a lot of trouble managing her classes and is always looking frazzled. She teaches two classes of general math and three of pre-algebra. Melinda has a reputation of not working very hard and of trying to get out of doing anything above and beyond the basic requirements of her classes. She is the first one out the door at the end of the day and arrives just as the school bell is ringing—coffee in hand and papers falling out of her plan book.

Katie Kantwell is the library media specialist at Heritage. She has been there for years and has a wonderful rapport with everyone. She works hard and has earned the respect of the students and faculty. She is calm, never seems to get rattled and keeps her personal opinions to herself. The principal and the other teachers hope she will remain at Heritage until she retires.

Each semester, Katie sends out a newsletter on activities with which the library media center has been involved during the preceding semester. Katie uses it to jog her colleagues' memories about the library media center and its role in the building. She hopes that teachers will see what others are doing and how the library has played a part. Then, when they plan a project or report, Katie is sure to be involved.

Melinda has never brought her classes to the library media center for any reason. The collection is not particularly strong in math and related subjects but there are some basic reference tools and a small selection of biographies and books in the Dewey 510 category. There are also books on mathematical puzzles and a growing collection of computer works. This time when Melinda gets the newsletter she decides to avail herself of the services of the library media center. Melinda meets with Katie and explains her idea. She wants the students to come up with a two-page biography of a famous mathematician. The biography must have two pages of text, a bibliography with at least two sources, and a picture of the person. She gives Katie a list of the mathematicians and together they pick two times for each of Melinda's five classes to come to the library.

When the first class comes into the room, they sit down and Melinda sits down as well. The students appear to have no idea what they're doing in the library media center. Katie also appears confused. She goes over to Melinda and inquires how this is going to proceed. Melinda says that she thought that since this was Katie's room, she would let Katie run the show. Katie has picked out some basic sources to talk about, but assumed that the students would have already identified the mathematician they would research and would have a general understanding of the project. Katie isn't sure if the focus should be on finding the information or developing a search strategy to find the information. She takes a deep breath, smiles and begins.

Questions:

1. What went wrong here?

2. Did Katie get so caught up with the idea that Melinda was bringing her classes to the library media center that she didn't get a clear understanding of the project or her role in it?

3. Is it Katie's job to explain the project and Melinda's job to sit there?

4. Is explaining the project going to teach the students about the library and its services?

5. If Katie explains a few of the math reference works and reviews subject and keyword searching on the online catalog, is her responsibility over?

6. Can Katie save this project as well as her reputation and Melinda's?

32. LIBRARY MEDIA CENTER VS. COMPUTER LAB

Kitty Weston is the library media specialist at the George Laurel Middle School. She has been there for about five years. Although she earned her MLS about twenty years ago, Kitty has not always been a practicing librarian. Depending on her husband's job, she has been in a variety of geographic areas as a librarian, school teacher and business person. Kitty has a BA in history and a BS in elementary education. In addition to her MLS, she also has an MBA. She is very versatile with many different computer programs and operating systems. Kitty is certified in elementary education, business education, library media, and also holds both middle school and English as a Second Language endorsements. She is an enthusiastic worker and makes a great contribution wherever she is.

Robert Moses, the principal at George Laurel, has a dream: to make every teacher and student a computer-literate learner. He has written a grant that has put together a computer lab. The lab houses 30 Macintosh LCIII computers, assorted printers, four modems with phone lines, fax interfaces, four CD-ROM stations, an LCD panel for overhead display, white boards and a scanner. The hardware is the envy of the other schools in the district. The business teacher can run the lab with her eyes shut, but she has a full schedule of typing and business classes in the business classroom. Kitty can also run the lab with her eyes shut, but she is responsible for the library media center.

As it happens, the new Macintosh Lab is in the room next to the library media center. There is a connecting door between the two. Mr. Moses has the idea that Kitty will run both rooms. Her background and certifications enable her to teach business and library skills. He sees a natural connection between teaching the online catalog (even though it is on an IBM) and the Macintosh computer. He gives Kitty a schedule that is one-hundred per cent flexible and tells her to go to it.

Questions:

   1. Is teaching the Macintosh LCIII a form of user education?

   2. Is the marriage between the lab and the media center a natural one?

3. Isn't the Mac a type of reference tool? What about the CD-ROM products and the modem connections?

4. Can't Kitty teach CDs and online searching in the Macintosh Lab?

5. Is this the first step away from teaching print sources and into teaching online products?

6. Are there search strategies that are transferrable from the library media center's online catalog to the CD projects in the lab or to the services available through the modem?

III. High or Secondary School Media Centers

A. READERS' SERVICES

33. DEATH BY DRUGS

Johnny Johnson had been a good student in the Park High School—that is until last year, when his parents had divorced and Johnny had been sent to live with his older sister and her family. A few weeks after the dramatic changes in his life had occurred, the teachers in the school began to notice a difference in the junior's attitude toward his studies and his fellow classmates. The once cheerful and outgoing student became withdrawn and sullen, and had begun to alienate himself from his friends. His work in class was carelessly done, his homework was incomplete and he was frequently absent from school.

One day while Millie Dawson, the media specialist, was eating lunch in the staff room, the teachers' discussion turned to Johnny's problem. Millie joined the conversation and suggested that the teachers contact the guidance counselor about Johnny. They agreed, and just then the bell for the next period rang.

The next day the school received a call from Johnny's sister informing the principal that Johnny had died the night before from an overdose of drugs. When the morning paper arrived the story about Johnny was on the front page. The principal called together Johnny's teachers and the guidance counselor for a conference on ways of dealing with the situation in the school. He knew that the students would be upset and that a whole school approach would be in order.

Following arrangements for bringing in an educational psychologist to aid in counseling the students, one of the teachers mentioned Millie's concern from the preceding day. He suggested that Millie be added to the team and that she might be able to aid them in dealing with the students. The principal agreed and asked Millie to join them.

Millie met with the group and suggested a number of ways in which she and the Media Center could help. She volunteered to prepare a list of the media center's resources on drug abuse for the teachers to consult. She also mentioned that she would prepare an exhibit on the topic so that students using the media center could look at books and materials. Millie further volunteered to suggest titles of novels about drug abuse to students when they asked or seemed to be concerned about what had happened to Johnny. She also recommended that focus be placed upon the issue of divorce and its effect upon family members, particularly adolescents.

Millie's suggestions were accepted by the team and she set about preparing the lists, using her computerized catalog and the automated reference services housed in the media center. She was pleased to be part of the team, and considered bibliotherapy to be an important segment of her role as a media specialist.

Questions:

1. Did the team follow the proper procedures for dealing with the situation?

2. Did Millie use all the options within her role as media specialist bibliotheraphist?

3. If a teacher had not mentioned Millie's help, do you think she would have gone to the principal herself after learning of Johnny's death?

34. NEW BOOKS

In the Biessel High School, media specialist Mibong Kim has several hard and fast rules. One of those is not to put any new materials on the shelves until she reads or views them. She does this not to censor the titles, but to know the materials better. She feels that this is important for helping students select books.

Mibong also posts a list of those new resources and selected older titles so that students can use the self-help method if they want to, or when she is busy. She carefully notes that the titles listed are not recommendations, only titles that she has read. At the bottom of the list she mentions that the media center often holds other titles by the same author or on the same topic. In addition, she adds subject headings to fiction titles when she catalogs.

The students have responded well to the lists, and many of them head for that bulletin board as soon as they enter the media center. They like the idea that Mrs. Kim has personalized their library, and Mibong finds that the resources on the list are well used and circulate often.

Questions:

1. Do you feel that Mibong should read and/or view all the new titles?

2. Is this an efficient use of her time?

3. Do you think that Mibong could distribute those lists to the classrooms for use by the teachers?

35. BOOK TALKS

A number of years ago Fred King read a book that fired up his imagination. He had found it in the collection in his media center in the Halsted High School and had been so engrossed that he read it in one sitting. He shared it with his family, and they too were enthusiastic.

This led Fred to want to read other titles by the same author and then to spread the word to the students in his school. He used the usual display methods and recommendations to students who inquired about reading suggestions. But he wanted to go further.

It was while reading a library journal that Fred saw an article about book talking. It struck his imagination, and he decided that it would be the perfect vehicle for his wish to expand his recommendations of titles to students. Not being particularly theatrical, and knowing that high school students required extra stimulus to engage their attention, Fred followed the article with readings in books and viewing a video that gave suggestions on how to book talk.

Now that he knew what to do, Fred realized that the next step would be to involve the teachers in this endeavor. He decided to start with the tenth grade English teachers, and asked them to give him twenty minutes of a class period for a book talk on a mutually agreeable title. He found two teachers who were willing to participate in the plan, and Fred came into class one day after the teacher had prepared the class. He used his voice to create the sound effects for the story, and found that the students were enthralled. He told part of the story, and then left the students breathless when he stopped just short of the climax of the tale. He would not tell them the end of the story, but showed them the book and mentioned that it and others like it were available in the media center. He also told them a bit about the author, describing the creative process and biographical details. The hardest part was faced by the teacher, who had to restrain the students' excitement for the remainder of the period.

Questions:

1. Do you think book talks are an effective way of stimulating reading?
2. Could this technique be used in other subject disciplines?

36. NON-ENGLISH-SPEAKING

Three-quarters of the students in Ridge High School do not speak or have English as a second language. Abul Selim, the media specialist in the school, is concerned that very few of those students use the library, and that most are missing an important resource that could aid the transition to English.

With this on his mind, Abul decides to make use of the media center by non-English-speaking students one of his objectives for the year. He draws up a plan for publicity for the media center and includes advertising methods among his strategies.

The first step in his plan is to set up an exhibit of resources in the media center that could be used by those second-language students. He decides to focus first on the dictionaries in the reference collection and makes colored copies of the covers and title pages from different languages and mounts them on the bulletin boards around the room. Next, he adds copies of readers and novels, some of which are bilingual and a few in only the foreign languages. He circles the display with words of welcome in different languages, hangs finding devices around the outside of the exhibit, and puts many of the books on top of shelves to attract attention.

Abul's second plan involves notices to the teachers and the school administrators about the special materials in the media center that could serve as resources for instruction. He also includes mention of the exhibit and displayed titles.

Step three in Abul's plan includes notices to the parents. For this he enlists the aid of the principal, who supports Abul's idea and offers to distribute a newsletter including a section about the media center via the usual home-school mailing network.

Abul's plan is to interest the parents in supporting a dialogue with the school by encouraging them to use the same materials that are available for the students.

Questions:

1. Do you think Abul's plan to encourage parents to participate in reading the materials is feasible at the high school level?

2. Has Abul considered how the students and parents can use the resources?

B. INFORMATION SERVICES

37. SOURCE MATERIALS FOR A TERM PAPER

Several students were waiting outside the door when Janey Rodriguez opened the media center in the Centerville Regional High School. Their words came spilling out in unison as they asked for help in the latest assignment in their world history class. Mr. Duffy, their teacher, had assigned a term paper dealing with an historical event in a country in the non-Western world. He had specified that they use original documents and well-cited secondary sources.

The students knew the difference between the types of sources, but their concerns were over the method of retrieving those materials. In addition, they were upset because the paper was due in four weeks and they didn't feel the time was sufficient to conduct the necessary research.

Janey was pleased that the students had remembered her lessons on the different types of research sources, and decided that some direct action would calm the situation. She immediately set the students to defining the event they wished to study and assigned them some background reading on the topic in the encyclopedia. She wasn't as pleased with the requirements for original documents or the time restraints set by Mr. Duffy, and resolved to speak with him as soon as possible.

Once the students had placed their topics on paper, Janey had them list the types of sources that would be pertinent to their events. Next to the sources she asked them to indicate where they thought they might find those resources, based upon the discussions they had had in library study classes. She glanced over the finding locations and noted that some of the students had listed places such as out-of-state libraries and historical societies. Since Janey was concerned about the feasiblity of such research, she suggested that the students might check with Mr. Duffy on their progress before they went any further.

The students left in a quieter mood than when they had arrived, and Janey breathed a sigh of relief. She checked the school schedule and noted that Sean Duffy had a free period later that afternoon. After resolving to talk to Sean then, she turned to her other work of the day.

Questions:

1. Was Mr. Duffy's assignment realistic, given the limited time constraints and the fact that the students might not have easy access to the necessary sources?

2. Should Janey have warned the students about the possible difficulty of obtaining information, given the fact that original documents are not often available to students?

3. What happened to the interaction between Janey and Sean? Would Janey's approach have been different if they had discussed the assignment before it was written? Do you suppose the assignment would have been different if they had discussed it?

38. THE BATTLE OF HASTINGS

Yvonne Montegeaudo, one of the eleventh-grade English teachers, came into the media center and headed toward the computerized catalog. She searched for a filmstrip on the Battle of Hastings, and having no hits, looked for John Malanga. John was the media specialist, and having just satisfied a student's request, he greeted Yvonne warmly.

After exchanging some pleasantries John inquired about

Yvonne's search. He knew the extent of the filmstrip collection in the center, and mentally confirmed the lack of anything with suitable information. John then asked Yvonne if a book would help. She agreed, and they set out to see if they could find the information in a print source.

John remembered having seen a picture of the battle depicted on a tapestry, and so together they searched for items on tapestries in the catalog. They found several, and after looking in the books on the shelf, discovered one with the desired picture. Yvonne was pleased with the illustration, stating that it was perfect since the book she was using in class mentioned the Bayeux Tapestry. Using that information, John searched through some other books and found several pages of text about the tapestry.

Yvonne was happy to find the information, and brainstormed with John on the best way to use it. He suggested that she might wish to involve the students in the lesson and that perhaps one or more of them could prepare a report and show the picture on the opaque projector. Yvonne agreed with his suggestion and left with her notes on the book titles. With a broad smile she thanked John and told him she would report back on the lesson.

Questions:

1. Did John handle the situation in the best possible manner?
2. Was he correct in making suggestions on how to use the materials?
3. Can you think of any other sources for the information?

39. SEX EDUCATION

Marie Roux had always been willing to help the teachers in the Field High School as they prepared for their classes. Her media center contained materials on all topics in the curriculum, and that included sex education as taught in the health classes. One day Cliff Sheffield-Warman, the physical and health education supervisor, came to the media center and asked Marie for materials on current sexually transmitted diseases. Marie agreed to prepare a bibliography for Cliff, using the automated catalog and Infotrac to locate items both in the media center and in the literature that could be secured through electronic retrieval sources and interlibrary loan. She went through the sources and produced a ten-page list of references, noting the call numbers and locations of those that could be found in the Field Media Center. Marie was so pleased with her bibliography that she printed out enough copies for all the students in the classes. She sent them to Cliff and he distributed them to the teachers, urging them to give copies to the students when they discussed the topic.

Three weeks later, Cliff came storming into the media center, waving a newspaper clipping in one hand and a copy of the bibliography in the other. The clipping was a copy of an editorial in the local paper, and it condemmed the use of taxpayer money to prepare such "dirty materials." Cliff accused Marie of causing problems and demanded that she assume all the blame for the bibliography and go with him to the principal. Marie went with him and found that the school administrators were also upset. Marie was put on the spot and tried to explain her policy of service and how the project was a cooperative venture.

Questions:

1. Was Marie correct in agreeing to the project?
2. Should she have distributed that many copies for student use?
3. What should Marie do next?

40. USING *BOOK REVIEW DIGEST*

The students in Nancy Hughes' senior English classes were required to write book reports for their quarterly assignments. Nancy had always been interested in the library, and had stipulated that the students read books from the High School library. She felt that to be a good way to encourage her students to use the library and increase circulation.

Ina Rosario, the media specialist, was aware of Nancy's assignment, and helped the students select books that would be interesting to them. She also, with Nancy's assistance, explained to the students how to prepare book reports, using examples of outlines, formats, and previous assignments.

One day Nancy came into the library carrying a pile of student reports. She and Ina sat down and compared the papers. Most of them were about the same length, and followed the same form and general tone of discussion. Nancy suspected that the students had copied the reports from somewhere and that they were not original student work. She was also concerned that some of the titles did not seem to be ones that would be in the library.

Ina and Nancy set about to do some detective work, and quickly found that some of the reports were from books not in the library's collection. Using her librarian skills, Ina searched through the reference collection and looked through *Book Review Digest.* She discovered that the students had also looked through the *Digest,* and had copied the reviews for their reports, rather than doing original work. Ina had mixed feelings about that revelation; she was pleased that the students had remembered her mention of the *Digest,* but concerned that they had "overlooked" her discussion of plagiarism and her comments that the *Digest* was a finding tool.

Questions:

1. What should Nancy and Ina do next?
2. Do you have any suggestions on how to teach about the indexing tools and how to discuss plagiarism?

C. STUDY, SELECTION, AND EVALUATION OF REFERENCE MATERIALS

41. NETWORK SELECTION

Whitman High School has been facing budget cuts for the past few years. Callie Mae Serrano, the new media specialist at the school, has been told that the materials budget for the library will be cut this year. She is concerned about her ability to purchase titles for the reference collection, especially since she has recently become aware of some exciting new mediated resource tools.

Callie Mae is faced with a dilemma: how to spread out the funds to the best advantage. She makes an appointment with the principal to discuss her situation and tells him of her concern. He advises her to speak to other librarians with more experience; perhaps they can help. Callie Mae calls the county educational media organization and learns that the group will be meeting in two weeks. Callie Mae is invited to attend the meeting where she can discuss the issue of selection as an agenda item.

On the afternoon of the meeting Callie Mae is introduced and then asked to present her question to the group. A lively discussion ensues, and the membership resolves to create a network for selection of costly reference materials. Callie Mae is invited to join a committee to write procedures and guidelines for the network, and gladly agrees to help.

A policy statement and selection and use guidelines manual is produced. It provides for the criteria for selection and evaluation of reference materials, and includes regulations for the cooperative sharing of information from the reference sources among the county group. The manual becomes a model for other educational media organizations, and Callie Mae and the other media specialists are pleased to have found a way to maximize resource sharing.

Questions:

1. Did Callie Mae follow the proper procedures for solving her problem?
2. Do you think the solution of a network for selection will work?

42. BALANCING RACISM AND SEXISM

The curriculum at Masters High School has just been expanded to include a section on teaching about racism and sexism. Rich Erler, the media specialist, has been on the curriculum committee which planned for the change, and is now faced with the need to select materials for the media center on these topics.

Rich sees his first assignment to be one of deciding on a balance of types of materials on the topics. He outlines his options and divides them into categories of reference sources, circulating materials, and vertical file materials. He decides to concentrate first on the reference or non-circulating collection, figuring that some of those materials can guide him in selection of the circulating collection. He searches through selection reviews and solicits comments from fellow educational media specialists in other schools.

After comparing sources, he places orders for a few reference and encyclopedic works that he feels can be used for quick reference and should not circulate. He also orders a number of bibliographic tools that can be placed in the teacher reference section and can be used as selection guides for the rest of the collection. He is careful to make sure that the titles he selects include both print and non-print formats.

Next, Rich considers materials for the vertical file he maintains in the media center. He uses that file for collections of ephemeral materials and clippings on topics of current interest. He considers it an important part of the reference collection of the media center, and assigns the aide to the task of clipping articles and watching the mail for ads and other miscellaneous papers that might be pertinent to the topics of racism and sexism.

After these preparations Rich feels confident that the media center can respond adequately to requests from the students and teachers as the issues of the new curriculum are taught. Once again he has responded to the need to involve the media center in the activities of the school and to enhance his role as facilitator of learning.

Questions:

1. Did Rich follow the proper procedures?
2. Can you think of any other sources he might have considered for selection of reference materials?

43. PRINT VS. ELECTRONIC

Encyclopedias, dictionaries and fact books have traditionally been considered the basic tools of the reference collection. Many schools keep the newest editions in the reference collection and circulate the older editions or distribute them to classrooms. Murak Patel had learned that in his library classes and had used that practice in his media center in the Muller High School.

Now things were different. Murak had received mailings announcing new electronic reference tools and had seen demonstrations of them at library conferences. He wanted to be part of the modern age and had read of the advantages and positive results on student learning from the electronic encyclopedias. In fact, he had heard so much that he almost felt smothered by the blitz of information.

Where to turn? There were so many things to consider. One was cost—how much would it cost to purchase and set up the system? Could it be purchased by a grant or was there money in the budget to cover it? And what about his practice of passing on the older editions? With the electronic reference sources there were no print copies to turn to circulation. And what type of electronic sources should he select? Online data bases? CD-Rom-based computerized resources? Should these tools be networked? Murak had plenty of questions, and decided to launch an in-depth feasibility study before making a final decision.

Questions:

1. Did Murak Patel consider all his options?
2. What do you think of the practice of circulating older editions of encyclopedias?

44. DICTIONARIES FOR DIFFERENT LANGUAGES

Sook La is the media specialist for the Middletown High School. Middletown is an urban community with a very diverse population. At least twelve different languages and varying dialects are spoken by the students and staff, who come from a mix of racial and ethnic groups. Sook's latest problem has been the request of students and teachers for dictionaries for different languages in the school.

Since Sook feels rather strongly that the media center should be the home of at least a base copy of reference tools, her dilemma is the selection of appropriate dictionaries. She isn't sure how many different ones she should purchase for the center, or if she will be able to assist students and staff in using the ones she does acquire.

There is a reference selection policy for the media center and Sook decides to consult it. The manual does not provide specific answers to her questions on the quantity of reference tools, but it does state that the reference collection should adequately provide for quick answers to a variety of questions coming from the school population. Sook feels that this is sufficient guidance and she proceeds to place orders for dictionaries that cover the basic twelve languages spoken in the school.

Questions:

1. Do you feel Sook made the correct decision?
2. Is that a good statement in the selection policy?
3. Did Sook select enough dictionaries?

D. USER INSTRUCTION

45. WHOLE CLASS VS. INDIVIDUAL

The students in Bob Willis's class were in a quandary. They were freshmen in a biology course, and Mr. Willis had just presented them with an assignment requiring research about either a theory of biology or a famous biologist. He told them that the paper was to consist of ten to twenty pages and should be documented. When the students indicated that they either did not know how or had forgotten how to go about conducting the research, Mr. Willis told them to "ask the librarian."

So, ask they did. A few made their way to the library almost immediately and approached Herb Williams, the media specialist. They had different topics to work on, and Herb did his best to show each one how to conduct research using the resources of the library. A second group walked into the library during the following period, and asked for help. This time Herb inquired about the nature of the assignment. When the students told him, he realized that a major problem seemed to be developing. Rather than talk to each student individually, he asked them to look through encyclopedias while he went to see Mr. Willis.

Bob was working in the teacher's room during his prep period when Herb found him. Herb explained the difficulty of trying to teach each student how to utilize the library, and asked if it would be possible to use part of Bob's class period the next day for library instruction. He added that group instruction was most effective when the entire class had the same assignment and needed guidance in how to do research.

Bob agreed with Herb and they walked back to the library together. They told the students that library instruction would be part of the next day's class and that he would be happy to help all he could. The students were pleased, and thanked both Bob and Herb for their concern and consideration.

Questions:

1. Was Herb correct in his assessment of the need for whole class instruction in this situation?
2. What would be the next step in the process?
3. Did Herb handle the problem properly?

46. BIBLIOGRAPHIC INSTRUCTION FOR NON-ENGLISH-SPEAKING STUDENTS

Martin Luther King High School is located in an urban area with a mixed population of English and non-English-speaking residents. The student body consists of children of long-time residents and those of new citizens and some migrant workers. The school contends with discipline problems, pregnant teenagers, and drug users and sellers.

The teachers in the school are dedicated to trying to teach this diverse group of students. They support the efforts of Helen Lee, the librarian, as she supplies them with resources to supplement their instruction.

When Helen spoke to the teachers during a faculty meeting she addressed the need to provide the students with library instruction. She felt this was important since the students would need to know how to find information during their school careers and in the future. The problem she faced was how to go about it, given the vast differences in languages found in the student body and the fact that she would be teaching all the students, not just one class.

Helen suggested that perhaps library instruction could become a school-wide project, and that time could be set aside from all classes to allow groups of same-language-speaking students to attend the library class together. She also mentioned that it might be good to involve some parents who spoke different languages to participate in the instruction. The consensus of the teachers and the administrators was that this might be a viable solution to the problem, and agreed to investigate the necessary scheduling arrangements.

Questions:

1. Was Helen Lee's idea workable?
2. Do you agree that library instruction is important for the students, or is it sufficient for the teachers to supply materials for the students?

47. STATE HISTORY

Lincolnville tenth grade social studies students study their state's history. Jerome Weintrab, the media specialist, teaches them search strategy through two assignments that they have for that class. For the first brief assignment, the students are required to do research about a prominent state citizen and produce a brief written report.

The second assignment, a written and oral report on some aspect of the state, is much more extensive. After Jerome conducts a class on how to do research, they are given a blank pathfinder sheet on which they must keep track of their search strategy. He tells them that this is a diary or a log of their research and that they can use it for any other research report.

The students are to keep track of what resources they use and what they find. If they find nothing in a particular source, that is noted. They are to include full bibliographic information so that their final bibliography will be accurate and easy to complete. The students discuss the pathfinders and their search strategy after the first assignment, analyzing why they did or did not find information in a particular resource.

Questions:

1. Is this an effective way to teach research methods?
2. Can students carry over the pathfinder method to other projects?

48. TECHNOLOGY FOR STUDENT SUCCESS

All ninth-grade students at Cape Town High School are required to take a six-week course titled "Technology for Student Success." As part of this course, each student is to learn how to use electronic information sources. They work with CD-ROM encyclopedias and indexes, and conduct online research.

Elaine Owens, the media specialist at the high school, believes in having students use the "discovery method" for learning about those information sources. She has found that the students are very receptive to computers and adapt very readily to using them. She puts the students in groups of two or three and sets them at the computers with a specific information search assignment in hand.

Since the various searching tools have built-in instructions, Elaine feels that the students can proceed on their own, and she is pleased that the computers almost force the students to limit and explain their searches. She believes that the computer is much more "patient" than a live instructor, and corrects their errors in a non-threatening manner.

The students are even allowed to conduct a simple *Dialog* search, and she assists them as needed to perform at least one search using a full-text database available on *Dialog*.

Elaine has found however, that the staff at the high school are generally not as comfortable with using the technology. It is usually the fear of not knowing as much as their students that compels them to come to Elaine for assistance in learning how to do research electronically. She has found that her teaching skills are needed, and a one-on-one approach usually works the best. She is gradually converting the entire school to the "new" way of conducting research, and this pleases her as she fulfills her role as described in *Information Power*.

Questions:

1. Are Elaine's approaches correct?
2. Should Elaine offer a pre-searching strategy session to the students before they start their research?
3. What role should the print reference resources play in the research process in this library?

Appendices

A. *Library Bill of Rights*
B. *School Library Bill of Rights*
C. *Freedom to Read*
D. *Freedom to View*
E. *Access to Resources and Services in the School Library Media Center*
F. *AASL Statement on Confidentiality of Library Records*
G. *Statement on Intellectual Freedom*
H. Sample Library Media Center Selection Policy
I. Sample Library Media Center Policy for Re-Evaluation of Selected Materials

Appendix A

LIBRARY BILL OF RIGHTS

The American Library Association affirms that all libraries are forums for information and ideas and that the following basic policies should guide their services.

1. Books and other library resources should be provided for the interest, information and enlightenment of all people of the community the library serves. Materials should not be excluded because of the origin, background or views of those contributing to their creation.

2. Libraries should provide materials and information presenting all points of view on current and historical issues. Materials should not be proscribed or removed because of partisan or doctrinal disapproval.

3. Libraries should challenge censorship in the fulfillment of their responsibility to provide information and enlightenment.

4. Libraries should cooperate with all persons and groups concerned with resisting abridgment of free expression and free access to ideas.

5. A person's right to use a library should not be denied or abridged because of origin, age, background, or views.

6. Libraries which make exhibit spaces and meeting rooms available to the public they serve should make such facilities available on an equitable basis, regardless of the beliefs or affiliations of individuals or groups requiring their use.

—Adopted June 18, 1948. Amended February 2, 1981, June 27, 1967 and January 23, 1980, by the ALA Council.

Appendix B

SCHOOL LIBRARY BILL OF RIGHTS

The American Association of School Librarians reaffirms its belief in the Library Bill of Rights of the American Library Association. Media personnel are concerned with generating understanding of American freedoms through the development of informed and responsible citizens. To this end the American Association of School Librarians asserts that the responsibility of the school library media center is:

To provide a comprehensive collection of instructional materials selected in compliance with basic written selection principles, and to provide maximum accessibility to these materials.

To provide materials that will support the curriculum, taking into consideration the individual's needs, and the varied interests, abilities, socio-economic backgrounds, and maturity levels of the students served.

To provide materials for teachers and students that will encourage growth in knowledge, and that will develop literary, cultural and aesthetic appreciation, and ethical standards.

To provide materials which reflect the ideas and beliefs of religious, social, political, historical, and ethnic groups and their contribution to the American and world heritage and culture, thereby enabling students to develop intellectual, integrity informing judgments.

To provide a written statement, approved by the local Boards of Education, of the procedures for meeting the challenge of censorship of materials in school library media centers.

To provide qualified personnel to serve teachers and students.
—*Approved by the Board of Directors, American Association of School Librarians, 1969.*

Appendix C

FREEDOM TO READ

The freedom to read is guaranteed by the Constitution. Those with faith in free men will stand firm on these constitutional guarantees of essential rights and will exercise the responsibilities that accompany these rights.

We therefore affirm these propositions:

1. It is in the public interest for publishers and librarians to make available the widest diversity of views and expressions, including those which are unorthodox or unpopular with the majority.

2. Publishers, librarians and booksellers do not need to endorse every idea or presentation contained in the books they make available. It would conflict with the public interest for them to establish their own political, moral or aesthetic views as a standard for determining what books should be published or circulated.

3. It is contrary to the public interest for publishers or librarians to determine the acceptability of a book on the basis of the personal history or political affiliations of the author.

4. There is no place in our society for efforts to coerce the taste of others, to confine adults to the reading matter deemed suitable for adolescents, or to inhibit the efforts of writers to achieve artistic expression.

5. It is not in the public interest to force a reader to accept with any book the prejudgment of a label characterizing the book or author as subversive or dangerous.

6. It is the responsibility of publishers and librarians, as guardians of the people's freedom to read, to contest encroachments upon that freedom by individuals or groups seeking to impose their own standards or tastes upon the community at large.

7. It is the responsibility of publishers and librarians to give full meaning to the freedom to read by providing books that enrich the quality and diversity of thought and expression. By the exercise of this affirmative responsibility, they can demonstrate that the answer to a bad book is a good one, the answer to a bad idea is a good one.

We state these propositions neither lightly nor as easy generalizations. We here stake out a lofty claim for the value of books. We do so because we believe that they are good, possessed of enormous variety and usefulness, worthy of cherishing and keeping free. We realize that the application of these propositions may mean the dissemination of ideas and manners of expression that are repugnant to many persons. We do not state these propositions in the comfortable belief that what people read is unimportant. We believe rather that what people read is deeply important; that ideas can be dangerous; but that the suppression of ideas is fatal to a democratic society. Freedom itself is a dangerous way of life, but it is ours.

—*Excerpted from a joint statement by the American Library Association and the Association of American Publishers. Adopted June 25, 1953; revised January 28, 1972; January 16, 1991.*

Adopted September 15, 1992 by the New Jersey Library Association Executive Board.

Appendix D

FREEDOM TO VIEW

The *Freedom to View,* along with the freedom to speak, to hear, and to read, is protected by the First Amendment to the Constitution of the United States. In a free society, there is no place for censorship of any medium or expression. Therefore, we affirm these principles:

1. It is in the public interest to provide the broadest possible access to films and other audiovisual materials, because they have proven to be among the most effective means for the communication of ideas. Liberty of circulation is essential to insure the constitutional guarantee of freedom of expression.

2. It is in the public interest to provide for our audiences, films, and other audiovisual materials which represent a diversity of views and expression. Selection of a work does not constitute or imply agreement with or approval of the content.

3. It is our professional responsibility to resist the constraint of labeling or pre-judging a film on the basis of the moral, religious, or political beliefs of the producer or filmmaker or on the basis of controversial content.

4. It is our professional responsibility to contest vigorously, by all lawful means, every encroachment upon the public's freedom to view.

—Originally drafted by the Educational Film Library Association's Freedom to View Committee, and adopted by the EFLA Board of Directors in February 1979.

—Adopted by the American Library Association on June 28, 1979, and endorsed by the ALA Council on January 10, 1990.

—Adopted by the Board of Directors of the Association of Educational Communications and Technology on December 1, 1979.
—Adopted by the Executive Board of the New Jersey Library Association on December 17, 1981.

Appendix E

ACCESS TO RESOURCES AND SERVICES IN THE SCHOOL LIBRARY MEDIA PROGRAM

An Interpretation of the Library Bill of Rights.

The school library media program plays a unique role in promoting intellectual freedom. It serves as a point of voluntary access to information and ideas and as a learning laboratory for students as they acquire critical thinking and problem solving skills needed in a pluralistic society. Although the educational level and program of the school necessarily shape the resources and services of a school library media program, the principles of the LIBRARY BILL OF RIGHTS apply equally to all libraries, including school library media programs.

School library media professionals assume a leadership role in promoting the principles of intellectual freedom within the school by providing resources and services that create and sustain an atmosphere of free inquiry. School library media professionals work closely with teachers to integrate instructional activities in classroom units designed to equip students to locate, evaluate, and use a broad range of ideas effectively. Through resources, programming, and educational processes, students and teachers experience the free and robust debate characteristic of a democratic society.

School library media professionals cooperate with other individuals in building collections of resources appropriate to the developmental and maturity levels of students. These collections provide resources which support the curriculum and are consistent with the philosophy, goals, and objectives of the school district.

Resources in school library media collections represent diverse points of view and current as well as historic issues.

Members of the school community involved in the collection development process employ educational criteria to select resources unfettered by their personal, political, social, or religious views. Students and educators served by the school library media program have access to resources and services free of constraints resulting from personal, partisan, and doctrinal disapproval. School library media professionals resist efforts by individuals to define what is appropriate for all students or teachers to read, view, or hear.

Major barriers between students and resources include: imposing age or grade level restrictions on the use of resources, limiting the use of interlibrary loan and access to electronic information, charging fees for information in specific formats, requiring permission from parents or teachers, establishing restricted shelves or closed collections, and labeling. Policies, procedures and rules related to the use of resources and services support free and open access to information.

The school board adopts policies that guarantee student access to a broad range of ideas. These include policies on collection development and procedures for the review of resources about which concerns have been raised. Such policies, developed by persons in the school community, provide for a timely and fair hearing and assure that procedures are applied equitably to all expressions of concern. School library media professionals implement district policies and procedures in the school.

—Adopted July 2, 1986 by the ALA Council.

Appendix F

AASL STATEMENT ON CONFIDENTIALITY OF LIBRARY RECORDS

The members of the American Library Association, recognizing the right to privacy of library users, believe that records held in libraries which connect specific individuals with specific resources, programs, or services, are confidential and not to be used for purposes other than routine record keeping; i.e. to maintain access to resources, to assure that resources are available to users who need them, to arrange facilities, to provide resources for the comfort and safety of patrons, or to accomplish the purposes of the program or service. The library community recognizes that children and youth have the same rights to privacy as adults.

Libraries whose record keeping systems reveal the names of users would be in violation of the confidentiality of library record laws adopted in many states. School library media specialists are advised to seek the advice of counsel if in doubt about whether their record keeping systems violate the specific laws in their states. Efforts must be made within the reasonable constraints of budgets and school management procedures to eliminate such records as soon as reasonably possible.

With or without specific legislation, school library media specialists are urged to respect the rights of children and youth by adhering to the tenets expressed in the Confidentiality of Library Records Interpretation of the Library Bill of Rights and the ALA Code of Ethics.

—ALA Policy 52.5, 54.15

Appendix G

STATEMENT ON INTELLECTUAL FREEDOM

The Association for Educational Communications and Technology.

The First Amendment to the Constitution of the United States is a cornerstone of our liberty, supporting our rights and responsibilities regarding free speech both written and oral.

The Association for Educational Communications and Technology believes this same protection applies also to the use of sound and image in our society.

Therefore, we affirm that:

Freedom of inquiry and access to information—regardless of the format or viewpoints of the presentation—are fundamental to the development of our society. These rights must not be denied or abridged because of age, sex, race, religion, national origin, or social or political views.

Children have the right to freedom of inquiry and access to information; responsibility for abridgement of that right is solely between an individual child and the parent(s) of that child.

The need for information and the interests, growth, and enlightenment of the user should govern the selection and development of educational media, not the age, sex, race, nationality, politics, or religious doctrine of the author, producer, or publisher.

Attempts to restrict or deprive a learner's access to information representing a variety of viewpoints must be resisted as a threat to learning in a free and democratic society. Recognizing that within a pluralistic society efforts to censor may exist, such challenges should be met calmly with proper respect for the beliefs of the challengers. Further, since attempts to censor sound and image material frequently arise out of misunderstanding of the rationale for using these formats, we shall attempt to help both user and censor to recognize the purpose and dynamics of communication in modern times regardless of the format.

The Association for Educational Communications and Technology is ready to cooperate with other persons or groups committed to resisting censorship or abridgement of free expression and free access to ideas and information.

—Adopted by: AECT Board of Directors, Kansas City, April 21, 1978

Appendix H

SAMPLE LIBRARY MEDIA CENTER SELECTION POLICY

The selection philosophy of the Princely Public Schools' Library Media Centers is to provide a wide range of learning resources at varying levels of difficulty with diversity of appeal and presentation of different points of view to meet the needs of our community of learners. The Library Media Specialist is charged with providing leadership and expertise—both necessary to assure that the school's library media program is an integral part of the school's instruction program.

It is the belief of Princely Public Schools that no document is final but is, rather, evolutionary. As such, the selection policy that follows will be reviewed and revised periodically.

INTRODUCTION

The selection policy which follows reflects and supports the principles of Intellectual Freedom described in the Library Bill of Rights (ALA), Freedom to Read (ALA and AAP), Access to Resources and Services in the School Library Media Program: An Interpretation of the Library Bill of Rights (AASL), and the Statement on Intellectual Freedom (AECT). Copies of these documents may be found at each of the school library media centers in Princely and also in the offices of the District Library Media Supervisor.

OBJECTIVES OF SELECTION

1. Each individual school holds the responsibility for building its collection to meet the needs and interests of its community of learners, including students, faculty, families, and staff.

2. In selecting information resources the library media specialist and the community of learners must consider both the internal holdings and those newly available information services. This is to guarantee that newer forms of technology and information sources be incorporated at the appropriate time and in accordance with curricular needs.

3. Each school is responsible for the selection of materials for the library media collection, by purchase, gift, or local production. The selection of materials follows established Princely Public School Department budget and ordering procedures as well as state and national guidelines.

4. The library media specialist must systematically conduct a needs assessment and evaluate the collection through such means as collection mapping, to assure that resources are selected and removed according to the principles of intellectual freedom. Care must be taken to provide students with access to information that represents diverse points of view in a pluralistic society.

RESPONSIBILITY FOR SELECTION OF LEARNING RESOURCES

The Princely Public School Board delegates the responsibility for the selection of learning resources to the professional staff employed by the school system. The District Library Media Supervisor sets acquisition processes including ordering procedures and processing of all materials. Collection development planning occurs at the school level.

While selection of learning resources involves many people (library media specialists, teachers, administrators, students, family members, and community persons) the responsibility for coordinating the selection of materials and making the recommendations for purchase rests with the library media specialist and the professional personnel at the building and district levels.

CRITERIA FOR SELECTION

1. Resources shall support and be consistent with the mission and goals of the Princely Public School Department and the aims and objectives of individual schools and specific curricula.

2. Learning resources shall meet high standards of quality in content and presentation.

3. Learning resources shall be appropriate for the subject area and for the age and developmental levels of the intended audience.

4. Learning resources shall have aesthetic, literary and/or social values.

5. Physical format and appearance of learning resources shall be suitable for their intended use.

6. Learning resources shall be designed to help the community of learners gain an awareness, appreciation, and knowledge of our diverse society.

7. Learning resources shall be designed to motivate students and staff to examine their own attitudes and behaviors so they may comprehend their own duties, responsibilities, rights, and privileges in relationship to the world around them.

8. Learning resources shall be selected for their strengths rather than rejected for their weaknesses.

9. Learning resources shall be selected to promote a balanced collection that should include opposing viewpoints on various issues, beliefs, and practices.

QUESTIONS:

1. Does this document provide general guidelines for the selection of all materials or just for library materials?

2. Can it be used for both? Why or why not?

3. Are the objectives for the selection of materials clearly stated? How can they be improved?

4. Are the lines of authority and responsibility clearly defined?

5. Do you agree that each school should select/build for their school? If Princely is an urban area is this cost effective? Should this section speak to cooperative collection development?

6. Although the policy refers to materials in various formats, should there be something specific for online products and searches that are printed out for student use?

7. Are the guidelines for selection and re-evaluation of titles in the existing collection clear? Should they be more specific? Should they be modified? How so?

Appendix I

SAMPLE LIBRARY MEDIA CENTER POLICY FOR RE-EVALUATION OF SELECTED MATERIALS

From time to time, the suitability of particular print and non-print materials may be questioned. The principals of freedom and professional selection must be adhered to, and the school will have no obligation to remove questioned material from use before or during a review process. If materials are questioned, the following procedure, based upon the American Library Association's national accepted policies will be followed.

1. The Requestor will submit his or her concerns in writing using the attached form, Request for Reconsideration of Library/ Media Center Materials. This form will be available in any of the following locations: the school principal's office, the office of the school library media specialist, or the office of the District Library Media Supervisor. Upon receipt of the completed form the building principal will notify the District Library Media Supervisor of the challenge, as well as either the Assistant Superintendent for Elementary Schools or the Assistant Superintendent for Secondary Schools.

2. The questioned material will then be reviewed by a committee of five members appointed by the building principal and his or her designee. This committee will be known as The Review Committee and be composed of the following building personnel:
- The Library Media Specialist
- Not more than two teachers

- The principal
- Not more than two parents from the building involved
3. The Review Committee will:
   - Examine the material in its entirety
   - Read reviews of the challenged material and investigate the acceptance of this material by other professional educators.
   - Judge the material for its strength and value as a whole and not in part—the impact of the entire work often being more important than isolated words, phrases, or incidents.
   - Submit a written report of their recommendations to the building principal with copies to the District Library Media Supervisor and the appropriate Assistant Superintendent.

4. The principal will notify the Requester of the decision of The Review Committee. This will be done in writing within 30 days of receipt of the complaint.

5. If the Requester is not satisfied with The Review Committee's decision, he or she may file a written appeal to the School Board. The School Board will consider the recommendations of The Review Committee and in consultation with the School Board Attorney, render a decision. This decision as to the suitability of the questioned material(s) will be made within 45 days of receiving the request for appeal. The School Board's decision will be the final decision within the Princely Public Schools.

REQUEST FOR RECONSIDERATION OF LIBRARY MEDIA MATERIALS PRINCELY PUBLIC SCHOOL DEPARTMENT

SCHOOL _____

REQUEST MADE BY _____

STREET ADDRESS _____

CITY/STATE _____ ZIP _____

TELEPHONE _____ REPRESENTING _____

PLEASE CHECK TYPE OF MATERIAL

_____ BOOK _____ PERIODICAL _____ KIT

_____ AUDIO _____ RECORD _____ FILM

CASSETTE _____ FILMSTRIP _____ PAMPHLET

_____ VIDEO

CASSETTE

_____ OTHER (BE SPECIFIC) _____

TITLE _____

AUTHOR _____

PUBLISHER _____

OTHER INFORMATION FROM THE ITEM _____

The following questions are to be answered by the Requester. If sufficient space is not provided, attach additional sheets. Please sign your name and date each of the attachments you supply.

1. DID YOU READ, LISTEN TO, OR VIEW THE ENTIRE WORK?

_____ YES _____ NO IF NO, WHICH SECTIONS?

2. TO WHAT IN THE MATERIAL DO YOU OBJECT? BE SPECIFIC, CITING PAGES, FRAMES IN A FILMSTRIP, FILM SEQUENCES AND SO ON.

3. WHAT DO YOU BELIEVE IS THE THEME OR PURPOSE OF THIS MATERIAL?

4. DO YOU FEEL THERE IS ANYTHING OF VALUE IN THIS MATERIAL? _____

_____

5. WHAT DO YOU FEEL MIGHT BE THE RESULT OF A STUDENT USING THIS MATERIAL? _____

_____

6. FOR WHAT AGE GROUP WOULD YOU RECOMMEND USING THIS MATERIAL? _____

_____

7. HAVE YOU HAD THE OPPORTUNITY TO REVIEW THE EVALUA-TIONS OF THIS MATERIAL BY PROFESSIONAL CRITICS?
   _____ NO _____ YES

8. IF YOU HAVE ANSWERED YES TO NUMBER 7, PLEASE LIST THE REVIEW YOU HAVE READ. _____

_____

9. WHAT DO YOU WANT THE SCHOOL TO DO ABOUT THIS WORK?
   _____ DO NOT ASSIGN OR RECOMMEND IT TO MY CHILD
   _____ WITHDRAW IT FROM ALL STUDENTS
   _____ SEND IT BACK TO THE LIBRARY MEDIA SPECIALIST FOR RE-EVALUATION
   _____ OTHER (BE SPECIFIC) _____

_____

10. WHAT WORK OF SIMILAR VALUE, CONTENT, AND FORMAT WOULD YOU SUGGEST TO REPLACE THIS MATERIAL? _____

_____

PLEASE SIGN AND DATE THIS FORM AND RETURN IT TO THE PER-SON WHO GAVE IT TO YOU.

_____

YOUR NAME   DATE

QUESTIONS:

1. By having the Requestor submit everything in writing, are they limiting complaints to the more literate members of the community?

2. Should there be a vehicle for interviewing the Requestor?

3. Should the deliberations of The Review Committee be open?

4. Why is the School Board Attorney involved only at the level of the School Board? Is it necessary that this person be involved from the beginning?

5. Should this procedure and the form be available in other languages?

6. Should there be an advocate for the Requestor who can provide translation service?

7. Should there be a statement made to the Requestor prior to the meeting of The Review Committee regarding why this material was added to the collection?

Bibliographies

A. Works Cited
B. Reference Methods and Philosophy, K–12: A Selected
   Bibliography
C. Professional Resources
D. Recommended Selection Tools

A. Works Cited

Aiello, Barbara. *Friends for Life.* Frederick, MD: 21st Century Books, 1988.

Banks, Lynne Reid. *The Indian in the Cupboard.* Garden City, NY: Doubleday & Company, 1980.

Blume, Judy. *The One in the Middle Is the Green Kangaroo.* New York: Dell, 1992.

Book Review Digest. New York: H.W. Wilson, annual. (1906–).

"Books and jobs challenged in two censorship cases," *School Library Journal,* May 1994, p. 12.

Buscaglia, Leo. *The Fall of Freddie the Leaf.* New York: Slack, distributed by Holt, 1982.

Children's Magazine Guide. New Providence, NJ: Bowker.

Fleischman, Sid. *The Whipping Boy.* New York: Greenwillow, 1986.

Grogan, D. *Practical Reference Work.* New York: Saur, 1979.

Infotrac. Foster City, CA: Information Access Co., 1991– .

Kerr, Judith. *When Hitler Stole Pink Rabbit.* New York: Dell, 1987.

Loh, Morag. *Tucking Mommy In.* New York: Orchard Books, 1988.

Macaulay, David. *Pyramid.* Boston, MA: Houghton Mifflin, 1975.

"Montana meets the Middle Ages," *New York Times,* March 14, 1994, p. 12.

Rylant, Cynthia. *Henry and Mudge and the Careful Cousins.* New York: Macmillan, 1994.

Schwartz, Alvin, ed. *Scary Stories to Tell in the Dark.* New York: Harper Collins, 1986.

Stine, R. L. *The Baby-Sitter.* New York: Scholastic, 1989.

——— *Baby-Sitter II.* New York: Scholastic, 1991.

——— *Baby-Sitter III.* New York: Scholastic, 1993.

B. Reference Methods and Philosophy, K-12: A Selected Bibliography

Aversa, Elizabeth. "Beyond search technique and strategy: helping students to be informed." *School Library Media Activities Monthly,* v. 8, pp. 30–31, 50, Sept. 1991.

Aversa, Elizabeth, et al. "Management of online search services in schools" (book review). *Wilson Library Bulletin,* v. 63, pp. 124–5, May 1989.

A basic reference collection for school library media centers. Austin: Texas Education Agency, 1990. ED336119.

Beaubien, Denise M., et al. "Software for patron use in libraries." *Library Trends,* v. 40, no. 1, pp. 1–197, Summer 1991.

Blandy, Susan Griswold, Lynne M. Martin, and Mary L. Strife, eds. *Assessment and accountability in reference work.* New York: Haworth Press, c1992.

Buboltz, Dale, et al. "Teaching library skills for the 1990s." *Book Report,* v. 10, no. 3, pp. 13–15, 17, Nov.–Dec. 1991.

Chatton, Barbara. *Reference services in the school media center.* Ohio Educ. Library/Media Assn., Higher Educ. Div., 1988.

Christensen, John O. *Reference services for school libraries in the 1980s: a selective bibliography.* Monticello, Ill: Vance Bibliographies, 1989.

De Silva, Rufus. *Developing the secondary school library resource centre.* London: Kegan Paul, 1993.

Fish, Bonnie, and Pat Walker "Introduction to reference—'80's style." *Show-me Libraries,* v. 40, pp. 14–16, Fall 1988.

Graef, Robert, et al. "Selection skills and collection development in school libraries." *Book Report,* v. 9, no. 2, pp. 14–15, 17, 19, 23–39, Sep.–Oct. 1990.

Hamilton, Donald. "On the other hand: like a pen without ink." *School Libraries in Canada,* v. 9, pp. 9–10, Spring 1989.

Information power: guidelines for school library media programs. Chicago: American Library Association and the AECT, 1988.

Jacobson, Frances F. "Information retrieval systems and youth: a review of recent literature." *Journal of Youth Services in Libraries,* v. 5, no. 1, pp. 109–13, Fall 1991.

Kohn, Rita T. *Have you got what they want?: Public relations strategies for the school library/media specialist: a reference tool.* Metuchen, N.J.: Scarecrow Press, 1990.

Mathews, Virginia H, et al. "Kids need libraries: school and public libraries preparing the youth of today for the world of tomorrow." *School Library Media Annual,* v. 9, pp. 228–38, 1991.

Mendrinos, Roxanne-Baxter. "CD-ROM and at-risk students: a path to excellence." *School Library Journal,* v. 38, no. 10, pp. 29–31, Oct. 1992.

Patrick, Gay D. *Building the reference collection: a how-to-do-it manual for school and public librarians.* New York: Neal-Schuman, 1992.

Problem definition process: a guide to research strategies. Harrisburg: Pa. State Library, 1989.

Rothstein, Samuel. "The school library as an information centre." *The Reference Librarian,* no. 25–26, pp. 157–60, 1989.

Valenza, Joyce Kasman. "The joy of searching (teaching online searching)." *Book Report,* v. 11, pp. 26–6, Sept./Oct. 1992.

Wreath, April, et al. "Technology and librarianship" *North Carolina Libraries,* v. 47, no. 3, pp. 136–7, 139–53, 155–61, Fall 1989.

C. Professional Resources

Buchanan, Jan. *Flexible Access Library Media Programs*. Libraries Unlimited, 1991.

Burress, Lee. *Battle of the Books: Literary Censorship in the Public Schools, 1950–1985*. Scarecrow Press, 1989.

Cianciolo, Patricia J. *Picture Books for Children*. 3rd ed. ALA, 1990.

Curriculum: The School Librarian's Role. Linworth, 1990.

Dame, Melvina A. *Serving Linguistically and Culturally Diverse Students: Strategies for the School Library Media Specialist*. Neal Schulman, 1992.

Gillespie, John T. and Spirt, Diana. *Administering the School Library Media Center*. 3rd ed. Bowker, 1992.

Information Power: Guidelines for School Library Media Programs. ALA, 1988.

Intellectual Freedom Manual. ALA, 1989.

Karpisek, Marian. *Policymaking for School Library Media Programs*. ALA, 1989.

Loertscher, David V. *Measures of Excellences for School Library Media Centers*. (Drexel Library Quarterly 21, #2). Libraries, Unlimited, 1988.

Media Production and Computer Activities. Edited by Thomas H. Walker and Paula K. Montgomery. ABC-CLIO, 1990.

The Newbery and Caldecott Awards: A Guide to the Medal and Honor Books. 1993 ed. ALA, 1993.

Prostano, Emanual T. and Prostano, Joyce S. *School Library Media Programs: Success in the 90's*. In-Time, 1989.

Reading Motivation. Linworth, 1990. ISBN: 0–938865–03-X.

Recommended Videos for Schools. Edited by Beth Blenz-Clucas and Gloria Gribble. ABC-CLIO, 1991.

Reichman, Henry. *Censorship and Selection: Issues and Answers for Schools*. ALA, 1988.

Rudin, Claire. *The School Librarian's Sourcebook*. Bowker, 1990.

School Library Media Annual. Libraries Unlimited, 1983.

Selecting Materials for School Library Media Centers. 2nd ed. Dona J. Helmer, Compiler and Editor. ALA, 1993.

Smith, Jane Bandy. *Library Media Center Programs for Middle Schools: A Curriculum-based Approach*. ALA, 1989.

Stein, Barbara L. *Running a School Library Media Center: A How-to-do-it Manual for Librarians*. Neal-Schulman, 1992.

Tips and Other Bright Ideas for School Librarians. ABC-CLIO, 1991.

Van Orden, Phyllis J. *The Collection Program in Schools; Concepts, Practices, and Information Sources*. 2nd ed. Libraries Unlimited, 1995.

Walker, H. Thomas and Montgomery, Paula K. *Activities Almanac: Daily Ideas for Library Media Lessons*. ABC-CLIO, 1990.

Woolls, Blanche. *The School Library Media Manager*. Libraries Unlimited, 1994.

D. Recommended Selection Tools

ALAN Review. (Assembly on Literature for Adolescents). NCTE, 1979.

Adventuring With Books: A Booklist for Pre-K—Grade 6. 9th ed. Edited by Mary Jett-Simpson and the Committee on the Elementary School Booklist of the National Council of Teachers of English. NCTE, 1989.

Appraisal: Science Books for Young People. Children's Science Books Review Committee, 1967.

Book Links: Connecting Books, Libraries and Classrooms. ALA, 1991.

The Book Report: The Journal for Junior and Senior High School Libraries. Linworth, 1982.

Book Review Digest. Wilson, 1905.

Book Review Index. Gale Research, 1965.

Booklist; Includes Reference Books Bulletin. ALA, 1905.

Books for the Teen Age. New York Public Library, Committee on Books for Young Adults, 1929.

Books for You: A Booklist for Senior High School Students. 11th ed. Edited by Shirley Wurth. National Council of Teachers of English, 1992.

Booktalk 5! More Booktalks for All Ages and Audiences. Edited by Joni Bodart-Talbot. Wilson, 1993.

Bosch, Stephen, Promis, Patricia, and Sugnet, Chris. *Guide to Selecting and Acquiring CD-ROMs, Software, and Other Electronic Publications.* ALA, 1994.

Bulletin of the Center for Children's Books. University of Illinois Press, 1945.

Catholic Library World. Catholic Library Association, 1929.

Children's Book Review Index. Gale Research, 1976.

Children's Books: Awards and Prizes. Children's Book Council, 1969.

Children's Catalog. 16th ed. Edited by Juliette Yaakov with the assistance of Anne Price. Wilson, 1991.

Children's Magazine Guide. Bowker, 1948.

The Computing Teacher: Journal of the International Society for Technology in Education. International Council for Computers in Education, 1979.

Curriculum Review. Curriculum Advisory Service, 1960.

Database: The Magazine of Database Reference and Review. Online, Inc., 1978.

Dickinson, Gail K. *Selection and Evaluation of Electronic Resources.* Libraries Unlimited, 1994.

Digest of Software Reviews: Education. School and Home Courseware, 1983.

Dreyer, Sharon Spredemann. *The Best of Bookfinder: A Guide to Children's Literature About Interests and Concerns of Youth Ages 2–18.* American Guidance Association, 1992.

Educational Technology. Educational News Service, 1961.

The Elementary School Journal. University of Chicago Press, 1900.

The Elementary School Library Collection: A Guide to Books and Other Media, Phases 1–2–3. 19th ed. Edited by Lauren K. Lee. Brodart, 1994.

Electronic Learning. Scholastic, 1981.

Emergency Librarian. Rockland Press, 1973.

English Journal. National Council of Teachers of English, 1912.

Fakih, Kimberly Olson. *Literature of Delight: A Critical Guide to Humorous Books for Children.* Bowker, 1993.

Film & Video Finder. 3rd ed. National Information Center for Educational Media, 1991.

Filmstrip & Slide Set Finder. National Information Center for Educational Media, 1990.

Freeman, Judy. *Books Kids Will Sit Still For: The Complete Read-Aloud Guide.* 2nd ed. Bowker, 1990.

From Page to Screen: Children's and Young Adult Books on Film and Video. Edited by Joyce Moss and George Wilson. Gale, 1992.

Gillespie, John T. *Best Books for Junior High Readers*. Bowker, 1991.

————. *Best Books for Senior High Readers*. Bowker, 1991.

Gillespie, John T. and Naden, Corinne J. *Best Books for Children: Preschool Through Grade 6*. 4th ed. Bowker, 1990.

————. *Juniorplots 4: A Book Talk Guide for Use with Readers Ages 12–16*. Bowker, 1992.

Greene, Ellin. *Books, Babies, and Libraries: Serving Infants, Toddlers, Their Parents and Caregivers*. ALA, 1991.

High Interest-Easy Reading: A Booklist for Junior and Senior High School Students. 6th ed. Edited by William G. McBride and the Committee to Revise High Interest-Easy Reading of the National Council of Teachers of English. NCTE, 1990.

High/Low Handbook: Encouraging Literacy in the 1990s. 3rd ed. Compiled and edited by Ellen V. LiBretto. Bowker, 1990.

The Horn Book Magazine. Horn Book, 1924.

InfoTrack. Information Access, 1980.

Instructor. Instructor Publications, 1981.

Journal of Youth Services in Libraries. ALA, 1987.

Katz, Bill and Katz, Linda Sternberg. *Magazines for Libraries*. Bowker, 1992.

Kennedy, Day Ann, Spangler, Stella S., and Vanderwerf, Mary Ann. *Science & Technology in Fact and Fiction: A Guide to Children's Books*. Bowker, 1990.

————. *Science & Technology in Fact and Fiction: A Guide to Young Adult Books*. Bowker, 1990.

Kies, Cosette. *Supernatural Fiction for Teens: More Than 1300 Good Paperbacks to Read for Wonderment*. 2nd ed. Libraries Unlimited, 1992.

Kimmel, Margaret Mary and Segal, Elizabeth. *For Reading Out Loud! A Guide to Sharing Books with Children*. Dell, 1991.

Kuipers, Barbara J. *American Indian Reference Books for Children and Young Adults*. Libraries Unlimited, 1991.

Language Arts. National Council of Teachers of English, 1975.

Library Hi Tech Journal. Pierian Press, 1983.

Library Journal. Bowker, 1876.

Library Talk: The Magazine for Elementary School Librarians. Linworth, 1988.

Lima, Carolyn W. and Lima, John A. *A to Zoo: Subject Access to Children's Picture Books*. 4th ed. Bowker, 1993.

Lynch-Brown, Carol and Tomlinson, Carl M. *Essentials of Children's Literature*. Allyn & Bacon, 1993.

Magazines for Young People: A Children's Magazine Guide Companion Volume. 2nd ed. Bowker, 1991.

Malinowsky, H. Robert. *Best Science and Technology Reference Books for Young People*. Oryx Press, 1991.

March, Andres L. *Recommended Reference Books in Paperback*. 2nd ed. Libraries Unlimited, 1992.

The Mathematics Teachers. National Council of Teachers of Mathematics, 1908.

Media and Methods. American Society of Educators, 1969.

Media Review Digest. Pierian Press, 1970.

Middle and Junior High School Library Catalog. 7th ed. Wilson, 1995.

Miller-Lachmann, Lyn. *Our Family, Our Friends, Our World: An Annotated Guide to Significant Multicultural Books for Children and Teenagers*. Bowker, 1992.

More Exciting, Funny, Scary, Short, Different, and Sad Books Kids Like About Animals, Science, Sports, Families, Songs, and Other Things. Edited by Frances Laverne Carroll and Mary Meacham. ALA, 1992.

Multicultural Review: Dedicated to a Better Understanding of Ethnic, Racial and Religious Diversity. Greenwood Publishing, 1992.

Neill, Shirley Boes, and Neill, George W. *Only the Best: The Annual Guide to Highest-Rated Educational Software, Preschool—Grade 12*. Bowker, 1989.

The New Booktalker. Edited by Joni Richards Bodard. Libraries Unlimited, 1992.

Nichols, Margaret Irby. *Guide to Reference Books for School Media Centers*. 4th ed. Libraries Unlimited, 1992.

Peterson, Carolyn Sue and Fenton, Ann D. *Reference Books for Children*. 4th ed. Scarecrow, 1992.

Pilla, Marianne Laino. *The Best: High/Low Books for Reluctant Readers*. Libraries Unlimited, 1990.

Recommended Reference Books for Small and Medium-Sized Libraries and Media Centers. Libraries Unlimited, 1982.

Richardson, Selma K. *Magazines for Children: A Guide for Parents, Teachers, and Librarians*. 2nd ed. ALA, 1991.

Rochman, Hazel. *Against Borders: Promoting Books for a Multicultural World*. ALA, 1993.

Rosenberg, Betty and Herald, Diana Tixler. *Genreflecting: A Guide to Reading Interests in Genre Fiction*. 3rd ed. Libraries Unlimited, 1991.

Rudman, Marsha K., Gagne, Kathleen Dunne, and Berstein, Joanne E. *Books to Help Children Cope With Separation and Loss: An Annotated Bibliography*. Bowker, 1993.

Schon, Isabel. *Books in Spanish for Children and Young Adults: An Annotated Guide*. Scarecrow, 1992.

————. *Guide to Juvenile Books about Hispanic People and Cultures*. Scarecrow, 1991.

School Librarian's Workshop. Library Learning Resources, Inc., 1980.

School Library Journal; The Magazine of Children's, Young Adult, and School Libraries. Bowker, 1954.

School Library Media Quarterly. ALA, 1954.

Science and Children. National Science Teachers Association, 1963.

Science Books & Films. American Association for the Advancement of Science, 1965.

The Science Teacher. National Science Teachers Association, 1934.

Senior High School Library Catalog. 14th ed. Wilson, 1992.

Shapiro, Lillian L. and Stein, Barbara L. *Fiction for Youth: A Guide to Recommended Books*. 3rd ed. Neal-Schuman, 1992.

Sinclair, Patti K. *E for Environment: An Annotated Bibliography of Children's Books with Environmental Themes*. Bowker, 1992.

Slapin, Beverly and Seale, Doris. *Through Indian Eyes: The Native Experience in Books for Children*. New Society Publishers/New Society Educational Foundation, 1992.

Social Education. National Council for the Social Studies, 1937.

Technology & Learning. Peter Li, 1980.

Venture into Cultures: A Resources Book of Multicultural Materials and Programs. Edited by Carla D. Hayden. ALA, 1992.

VOYA: Voice of Youth Advocates. Scarecrow Press, 1978.

Your Reading: A Booklist for Junior High and Middle School Students. 8th ed. Edited by Alleen Pace Nilson. National Council of Teachers of English, 1991.

Zvirin, Stephanie. *The Best Years of Their Lives: A Resource Guide for Teenagers in Crisis.* ALA, 1992.

Index